COLLEGE STREET, PETERSFIELD

by Petersfield U3A

Published by Petersfield Museum

College Street, Petersfield

First published in the UK in 2015 by
Petersfield Museum
The Old Courthouse
St Peter's Road
Petersfield
GU32 3HX

Printed by
Sarsen Press
22 Hyde Street
Winchester
SO23 7DR

ISBN 978-0-9934528-0-2

Foreword

The Hampshire market town of Petersfield has evolved steadily since the 12th century into the delightful and attractive centre of today. The manner of change has been recorded in many different volumes of text and pictures, but these seem only to reveal the need for yet further works. The stories of the buildings in the High Street and The Square have already been produced by the Petersfield Area Historical Society and these have stimulated interest in other thoroughfares.

Some members of Petersfield U3A (University of the Third Age), many of whom had either lived in the town for much of their lives or chosen to spend their retirement here, shared that interest. From the common desire to discover more of the history of the town was born the local history group responsible for research and producing this publication. Early discussions confirmed that the most interesting and challenging topic seemed to be College Street, with its mix of old and new buildings, including the oldest house dating from the 14th century. The changing social structure over the years lent another level of interest to the story.

Membership of the U3A group changed over the period of study, but at monthly meetings research notes were shared. Visits were made to the homes of local people and beyond, and much time was spent in the Hampshire Record Office, Petersfield Library and the Petersfield Museum. Particular thanks are due to the Petersfield Museum for their co-operation in ensuring the publication of the finished product.

Whilst much of the content of this book is the result of hours of research by individual group members, whose names appear in the list of contributors, this book could not have been produced without the assistance of the residents of College Street. Special mention must also be made of Edward Roberts, author of *Hampshire Houses 1250–1700*, who has assisted with the dating of some buildings.

Although this publication is the tangible result of three years' work, the group's endeavours have proved most enjoyable and have stimulated much interest amongst members as well as creating new friendships.

Keith Hopper (Group Chairman)

Contributors

CONTRIBUTORS
Carole Hopper, Keith Hopper, Bill Gosney, Margaret Hawkes,
David Jeffery, Peter Jolly, Angela Robinson, Diana Syms

FORMER MEMBERS AND CONTRIBUTORS
Joan Fanshawe, Esther Jones, Ann Kersley, Margaret Mackay, Heather Mandow,
Teresa Murley, Marjorie Pither, Olivia Tottle, Jennie Woodward

EDITORS
David Jeffery,
Peter Jolly

PHOTOGRAPHY
Bill Gosney,
David Jeffery

PRODUCTION & COVER PHOTOGRAPHY
Tracey Howe

Special thanks go to the Hampshire Record Office for the images on pp. 8, 12, 18, 21, 48, 58, 62 and the maps on pp. 27, 28, and 53
and to Petersfield Museum for the images on pp. 1, 2, 3, 11, 34, 37, 38, 43, 52, 64

Sources

Every property in College Street will have undergone research into its history by reference to the following sources. Additional sources are listed at the back of the book.

Hampshire Record Office, Winchester
(historic records and photographic archives)
Petersfield Museum
(written records, other documents, photographs)
Petersfield Library
(material relating both to the town and to Hampshire generally)
The Petersfield Index
(listing all published material on Petersfield by local or other authors)

Further references and acknowledgments

These are listed at the end of the book under individual properties. All the contributors are extremely grateful for the information provided by a large number of people during the production of this volume.

Contents

Present-day Buildings

Histories

Maps

Book Layout

The book has been designed to cover the east side of the street first, from The Red Lion to Churcher's Old College, followed by the west side, from nos. 2 – 52a. Present-day buildings are described in the main texts. Historical buildings that are no longer visible are mentioned in the separate panels.

The Red Lion

Perhaps the most impressive, if not the oldest, building in College Street is "The Red Lion". Although it proudly presents its white rendered face to College Street, with its Georgian façade and Doric porch with fluted columns, it was historically more associated with the High Street, and its continuation into what is now Heath Road, but sometime Horn Lane. The present building dates from the early 18th century, at a time when the development of the Turnpike along what are now College and Dragon Streets increased the requirement for coaching inns such as the Red Lion. What is popularly regarded as the Red Lion has a complex history.

Since 1949, the inn has been a listed building, a listing that incorporates the formerly separate and lower two storey building fronting Heath Road, that was known as the Tap, the running of which has often been associated with the running of the Red Lion. On the southern first floor elevation of the Tap is an 18th century Sun Insurance mark. The car park for the inn is the site of a former brewery, and facing into that car park for the inn, and separated from it by a pair of gates is a nineteenth century construction, the Old Masonic Hall, which is also listed.

An indenture of 1st September 1620 describes the site as comprising three tenements. The larger was occupied by John Ruffen, a weaver, victualler and alehouse keeper, and the two smaller ones by Henry Stirt and Francis Hopkins. By 1654, the innholder was Jeremy (Jeremiah) Collyer, and in 1666 all three tenements were commonly called or known by the sign of the White Horse. By the 1680s the owner was Roger Goldring, a carrier and innholder. From his will written in 1703 it can be seen that to the north of the White Horse, on what had been the Bridge Garden (possibly a reference to a crossing of the Drum Stream) with stables and a workshop was built the Black Horse. When he died in 1705, a prosperous tradesman, he bequeathed the White Horse, where he lived, and which it is suggested was later to become "the Tap", to his widow and then to Elizabeth, daughter of his son Hillis.

The Black Horse was to pass to his infant granddaughter, Elizabeth Jacques. By 1729, she had married Richard Earwaker of Meonstoke, and it is recorded that the site on the corner of College Street and what is now Heath Road was the "The Sun Inn", in the occupation of William Burch. The ensuing few years are blessed with a plethora of surviving legal documents reflecting the changes on the ground. Part of the old tenements were pulled down, leaving in place "the Tap", and a more modern building was

constructed. By an agreement of December 1733, John Jolliffe, who had been assembling adjacent property had agreed to purchase the inn, still known as the Sun, but by the following year it had been re-branded as the Red Lion, a name that had hitherto belonged to the establishment on the diametrically opposite corner of the High Street.

For the remainder of the 18th century, and much of the 19th century, the Red Lion played an important role in the coaching trade, although its tenants came and went, the exception being Edward Patrick

The Antrobus Almshouses

When Thomas Antrobus of Heath House died in 1622, he stipulated in his will that his daughter, Elizabeth, with a bequest of one hundred pounds, should found "an almshouse or hospital for as many of the poor lone men and women as the money would provide." These worthies were to be selected by the occupants of Heath House and churchwardens. His friends, Mr. Barlow and Mr. Arthur Bold, were to be the trustees.

In 1624, they purchased a plot of land and built a stone almshouse with a gable-ended tiled roof and stone mullion casement windows. There was room for four "poor lone men and lone women" each having their own accommodation. No endowment was left for the maintenance of the building. This soon became a problem and as early as 1710 the building was referred to as "the old almshouse".

It is evident from the National Census records that a number of residents had relatives living with them and, in 1861, a Marah Hooker even had a "boarder". In 1880, the Trustees of the Almshouse Charity of Thomas Antrobus sold the Almshouses to Robert Luker. The investment of the acquired money was to then enable a weekly sum of two shillings to be paid to two elderly women chosen by the church wardens. The buildings were not pulled down but incorporated into the adjacent Lukers' Brewery, being used as a boiler house and a store.

By the early part of 20th century, the Antrobus Almshouses adjoining Lukers' Brewery were reported to be in a poor state of repair but, after the brewery fire of 1934, the building, by then minus its roof and upper floor, survived until the site was cleared for the widening of the road for a junction with the new Tor Way.

who stayed from 1789 to 1818. The estate map of the Jolliffe family produced in 1773 depicts the site with gates on the College Street side, giving entry to a large coachyard. In 1790 the hotel frontage onto College Street was rebuilt, in the form recognisable today. One aspect of the demand for accommodation and hospitality is reflected in an 1827 lease of the Tap, described as "of or belonging to the Red Lion", and is adjoined by a "building fitted up for the accommodation of soldiers quartered or billeted on the tenant." By then, John Atkinson had acquired both the Tap, which would potentially serve local drinkers, and the site of what was to become the Masonic Hall.

However, it is the name of the name of Robert Crafts which dominates the 19th century history of the Red Lion itself. His name appeared on the census return, aged 22, as the innkeeper in 1841, with his four sisters living with him. By 1857, he had also acquired and refurbished the Dolphin Hotel, and was advertising his services not merely as a brewer, hotelier and innkeeper, but also offering hearse and mourning coaches, as well as post horses and carriages. He operated "The Rocket" four-horse coach daily to the railhead at Godalming, and a thrice-weekly horse-drawn omnibus to Alton, again to meet Waterloo trains, as well as a daily service to Portsmouth. The coming of the London and South-Western Railway to Petersfield in 1859 sounded the death-knell of these services to railheads.

In 1873, the lease of the Red Lion passed from Robert Crafts to Messrs. J. and R. Luker, and, on 2nd April 1890, the freehold of the premises was also acquired by the Luker family, thus ending over 150 years of association with the property by the Jolliffes. John Luker died in March 1899, leaving the Red

Lion as part of his estate to his sister Sarah and his nephew William Luker. Lukers' period of ownership, expiring on the sale to Strong & Co of Romsey in 1933 of their entire interest in the site, is associated with the imposing, if not particularly elegant, six-storey tower to the brewery. Sited between the Red Lion itself and the Antrobus Almshouses, it was a dominant feature of the landscape until the disastrous fire of 1934 which, although leaving the Red Lion intact, destroyed the brewery. Subsequently on its site, now the inn car park, the brewers maintained an off-licence.

After Strongs sold out to Whitbreads, whether hotel or inn, the Red Lion has, over the past fifty years, had a number of re-incarnations, from a lease of April 1963 to J. Lyons and Company, to a Beefeater Steakhouse and a failed attempt in 2006 to create a conference facility. Since 2010 it has traded as a "Wetherspoons Inn" operated by J. D. Wetherspoon plc. Ironically, in view of the sale two hundred years previously to John Atkinson to facilitate an establishment without ties to any particular brewer, the Red Lion today boasts that it, too, is a Free House.

Lukers' Brewery

A building that has a footprint corresponding to that of Robert Crafts' Steam Brewery is shown on the Tithe Map of 1840. The freeholder of the land was William Jolliffe, and the Crafts family – Robert Crafts and his three sisters – were recorded as being the licensees of the Red Lion Hotel, on the same site, and the Dolphin Hotel opposite. By 1855, it seems that Robert Crafts owned both the hotels.

As early as 1878, Kelly's Gazetteer and Directory lists "Luker Bros; brewers, maltser & wine & spirit merchants, College Street." However, it is not until 1880 that Robert Crafts sells the brewery, for £7,604.8s.0d., to Mr. Robert Luker, but it was his eldest sons, William and Robert Charlwood, who ran it as a successful family business, serving eight public houses and hotels locally and trading as W. and R. Luker.

William's daughter, Betty Wardle, recalls in her book *Family Journey – the War Years* that, as well as the main brewery building, there was a six-storey high tower with a tall chimney protruding from the top; a boiler house and bottle store in the old almshouses; the brewery yard with a weeping willow in the middle and a low wall and ornamental railings on the A3 road side; the cooper's yard; an engineering shop for repairs; stables for the dray horses, a number of which were commandeered by the army in the First World War.

In the early thirties, when Robert died, and with increasingly stringent bye laws and restrictions being put on brewers, William decided to sell the brewery. He sold to Strong and Co. of Romsey on December 12th 1933. In 1934, Strongs transferred the brewing business to Romsey leaving the premises empty with all fittings and machinery removed. The company retained the adjoining off-licence and the Red Lion Hotel.

The site was then acquired by the Filer brothers, who intended to demolish the buildings to make way for a modern cinema. However, on the evening of Sunday August 26th 1934 a fire broke out, gutting most of the building but leaving the chimney and a small part of the tower. College Street had to be closed to traffic for a week for safety reasons whilst the remaining ruins were cleared. The off-licence survived until 1970 when it, too, was demolished for the construction of Tor Way.

The Home from Home Canteen

A canteen for the numerous troops passing through Petersfield during the Second World War had been opened in the Drill Hall in Dragon Street, but the building was soon required by the Home Guard. In May 1941, Hyman and Soloman Filer, who had previously purchased the site of the derelict Lukers' Brewery, leased part of its land to Kathleen Money-Chappelle and a band of volunteers for a period of five years or until six months after the signing of the armistice, whichever was the shorter.

The foundation stones for Mrs. Money-Chappelle's Home from Home canteen – a mainly wooden building – were laid in June 1941. Quickly built, it was officially opened that August, with a ceremonial march past. The numerous facilities it provided were eventually used by thousands of allied troops moving between Portsmouth and the camps in which they were stationed. It finally closed in July 1946.

By the end of the Second World War, there were about two hundred girls on the roll at Petersfield County High School for Girls at the end of the High Street. In the 1950s, when numbers had increased to 400, extra rooms had to be found, so the school took over the huts built for the "Home from Home" canteen to use as an annex.

The school used the buildings as a kitchen and dining room, but in addition there were two main classrooms, a small music room, two cloakrooms and toilets. The canteen area was also used as a sewing room and an assembly was held there each week.

The huts were vacated by the school when it closed in 1960 and remained unoccupied. By November 1976, the "Old School Canteen", still owned by the Filer brothers, was sold to The Secretary of State for the Environment for £35,000 to make space for the widening of College Street at its junction with the new Tor Way. The huts were pulled down, but the foundation stones, commemorating the original "Home from Home Canteen", were saved and are now resting at the foot of the west wall of the Festival Hall.

Kathleen Money-Chappelle

The foundation stones (right) reflect the cosmopolitan character of the canteen itself: they commemorate the British, Canadian, Australian and New Zealand troops who passed through its doors, who were often joined by Free French and Dutch Navy personnel, Czech and Polish troops, and Americans based in many parts of Hampshire.

KATHLEEN
MONEY-CHAPPELLE
FOUNDER / ORGANISER
GOOD LUCK
FROM THE
A.T.S. W.R.N.S. & W.A.A.F.S.
GOOD LUCK FROM
THE BRITISH FORCES
ARMY NAVY MARINES
AND AIR FORCE
THESE STONES WERE LAID BY MEMBERS
OF THE FIGHTING SERVICES
THEY WERE THE FOUNDATION STONES OF
THE HOME FROM HOME CANTEEN
AND SOCIAL CLUB IN COLLEGE STREET
BUILT AND OPENED IN AUGUST 1941
AND CONTINUED UNTIL JULY 1946
MANY THOUSANDS OF HOME AND OVERSEAS
TROOPS REMEMBER WITH GRATITUDE
THE WELCOME THEY RECEIVED THERE
GOOD LUCK
FROM
CANADA
GOOD LUCK
FROM
AUSTRALIA
GOOD LUCK
FROM
NEW ZEALAND

The Old Masonic Hall

In 1820, Hylton Jolliffe and his nominee, Baron Hotham, were returned as Members of Parliament for the Borough of Petersfield. This was unsurprising, as the pocket borough had long been cultivated by the Jolliffes, the principal landowners in the town. But the two losing candidates, amongst them Nathaniel Atcheson, a London attorney, challenged the result, albeit eventually unsuccessfully, and took their complaint both to a House of Commons Committee hearing and appeal. "The Petersfield Case", as it is often referred to, concerned the subdivision of plots and the "manufacturing" of voting rights, which indirectly led to the parliamentary reforms of the 1830s, substantially enlarging the male franchise and doing away with numerous "rotten boroughs". Locally, however, it had polarised political opinion. The Old Masonic Hall is intrinsically linked with the conflict between Hylton Jolliffe and the Atchesons.

The Jolliffe family held the freehold of The Red Lion, let out in 1789 on a thousand-year lease, and whilst the Old Masonic Hall today forms part of the Red Lion complex, and is joined to the Georgian elevations of the inn itself by a gateway arch leading into what was once the stable yard of the Inn, for a time it had a completely separate history.

The earliest known Masonic Lodge in the town was given a charter by the then Grand Master in 1821. The group of freemasons searched for suitable premises to conduct their business, and an indenture of 1822 recited their problems: they deplored the absence of any inn untied to any specific brewery. They also planned to raise £3675 and to construct a Hall or Lodge Room and to provide a Reading Room and Billiard Room. John Atkinson had recently acquired the Tap and the stables and lands behind, and now he also held the residue of the thousand year lease of The Red Lion.

This 1822 indenture, to which Nathaniel Atcheson and two other family members were parties, together with many other subscribers to the venture, transferred to John Atkinson and William Curling, trustees for the Lodge, both "The Tap", fronting onto what is now Heath Road (which provided the Free House for the benefit of the town's inhabitants) and the land behind. By no later than 1826, the Masonic Hall had been built on this land.

However, after this initial burst of activity, the Lodge fell on hard times and closed in 1838. But the 1860s saw a revival, and for a century thereafter the Old Masonic Hall, at the rear of the Red Lion, was the centre of freemasonry in the town. It appears that, notwithstanding its longevity, periods of growth were sometimes offset by stagnation and decline.

Despite the developments of nearly two centuries ago, the history of the building (and of the Tap), continued to be linked to the Red Lion itself, and the entire site has seemingly been in unified ownership or control since the times of the Luker family. Largely hidden from view by the brewery, it was unscathed by the brewery fire of 1934 and continued to be used by Lodge of Friendship No. 928 until fifty years ago. In 1933, the Masonic Hall had been held on a lease, but rising rents and costs associated with the premises were to become an issue a generation later. The lease was finally surrendered in June 1966, and the Lodge moved into the former Primitive Methodist Chapel in Windsor Road.

As for the Old Masonic Hall, when it was listed in 1973, it was described as a storeroom. It has not seemingly had any independent usage since. It is a two-storey brick structure, described as "mid-19th century" with a slate roof carried forward at the gable ends offering a pediment effect. Most visible to the passing observer is the northern elevation, with upper storey windows blocked, and, on the western elevation, the large first floor three-light Gothic type window, and double doors below it. Within the open upper storey of the building can still be seen an equivalent window in the eastern wall, blocked up by a later brick extension.

In 2006 an application for planning permission to convert the Masonic Hall and adjacent stable building to conference facilities was granted, but the permission lapsed, and, as can be seen from the signage on the gateway, it is now part of the Wetherspoons business operation.

Charlie Dickins' Garden

With the centenary of 1st Petersfield Scout Group due to be celebrated in 2007, their leaders were looking for a way to commemorate the event. The project to cultivate the derelict corner of Tor Way and College Street began when Hampshire Highways gave permission for the clearance of the overgrown eyesore. Flower beds were dug, bulbs donated by Scouts' and Cubs' parents and, in 2008, daffodils bloomed for the first time.

Other work has included organising the donation of a bench from Round Table, making a woodland walk at the rear, adding bird boxes and a mosaic made by the Cubs in 2012 for the Queen's jubilee.

The garden is named after Charlie Dickins (left), a local dentist who was a long-serving Scoutmaster with 1st Petersfield. The garden won Petersfield in Bloom environmental category in 2012 and, early in 2015, a time capsule was buried containing Group Scouting memorabilia in honour of a number of other long-serving leaders who had passed on.

Tor Way

The construction of Tor Way in July 1975 had a major effect on College Street. Prior to this, the street had been a source of much discontent for decades as the town was a major bottleneck on the A3 Trunk Road which ran from London to Portsmouth. Like many of the trunk roads in the post-Second World War period, its designation as a major route was at odds with its standards. As time progressed, different lengths of the once narrow two-way road were improved and, when these were eventually joined up, they created the new dual carriageway that is in use today, by-passing all of the towns. Petersfield's by-pass was opened in 1992.

The early College Street, known as Stoneham Street, had no footways and was merely a shared space for all wheeled transport, horses, livestock and humans, but the eventual introduction of mechanical transport, cars and bicycles led to the necessary segregation of pedestrians onto footways and the restriction of road width for everyone else. Throughout its length, College Street was basically a narrow two-way street and the old A3 traffic had to travel down Ramshill, pass through the gap in the embankment where the railway bridge for the Petersfield - Midhurst Railway had stood, turn right into Station Road, then sharp left into College Street.

Tor Way was conceived as a one-way gyratory system to remove most of the conflicts and delays and has been a major success in keeping traffic moving on the east side of the town centre. Unfortunately, in the process of constructing Tor Way, the town had to lose some of its heritage: the Lukers' Brewery buildings (derelict since the fire in 1934), the "Home from Home" canteen, The Pines and the farmhouse "Thurston" were all demolished to make way for it. It also enabled other developments to proceed, however, as access to "The Village" (Grenehurst Way) and indeed the Herne Farm Estate would have been very different, if not impossible, without it.

After the arrival of the by-pass, there was a short period when College Street was closed to traffic to allow enhancement works to take place and these have transformed the street into a low speed, pedestrian-friendly area. Perhaps inevitably, this has led to calls for all-through traffic to be removed by converting Tor Way into a two-way road. Whilst this would be very desirable for College Street residents and businesses, there are serious issues regarding traffic flows and delays and such a scheme is unlikely to be realised. It would require major works to take place at each of the main junctions on College Street, Tor Way and Station Road, with the high risk that congestion would be worse at peak hours and the street scene badly scarred by traffic signals, signs, wider roads and queues of traffic.

The Cedar of Lebanon c.1760

The Petersfield Demonstration Project

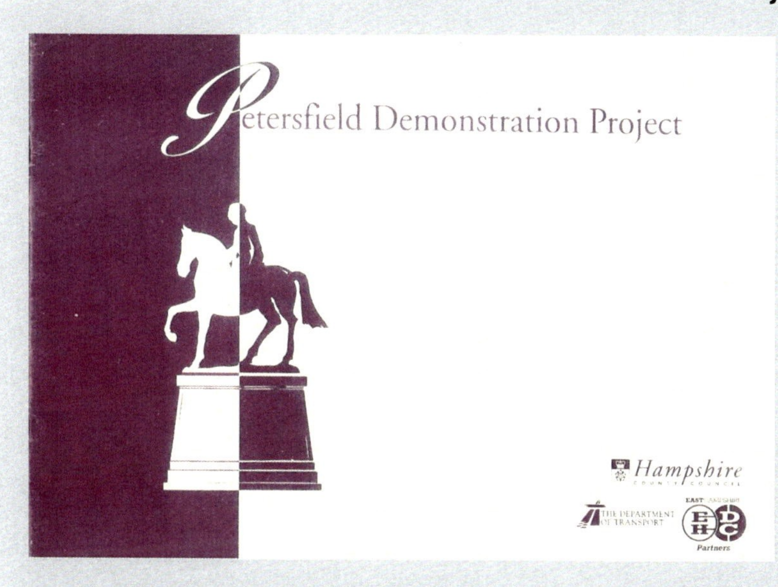

The completion of the town's 12 mile by-pass in July 1992 was to be shortly followed by an offer from the Department of the Environment to fund a "Demonstration Project". This scheme offered to six small towns nationwide was intended to show the environmental benefits for town centres which could result from a by-pass.

In Petersfield, the first phase of the £2m project brought an attractive enhancement to Dragon Street. The scheme produced a visually improved street scene: pavements were widened with old-style paving slabs, rumble strips were inserted in the roadway to slow traffic down, the war memorial was enhanced as a focal point by creating a new paving pattern, lay-bys for buses and parking were incorporated into the tree-lined pavements and space was created for a town mosaic celebrating the completion of the by-pass. This first phase of the Demonstration Project was completed in 1993 and the second phase, the remodelling of College Street – similar to that effected in Dragon Street – began and was completed in 1995.

The third and final phase, never to be undertaken, was to have been one of those sporadic attempts to re-route traffic away from College Street by making Tor Way into a two-way road.

Malcolm Rifkind, the former Secretary of State for Transport, explained the ethos behind these projects: "Bypasses in themselves achieve great environmental benefits by redirecting traffic to more suitable routes. A new bypass can have a much bigger impact on the quality of the local environment if complementary measures are implemented at the same time which take advantage of the fresh opportunities which arise if through traffic is removed or significantly reduced. These opportunities can include the introduction of traffic calming measures, improved provision for pedestrians, cyclists and other vulnerable road users, landscaping and environmental enhancements."

The project management team for Petersfield (the Department of Transport, Hampshire County Council, and East Hampshire District Council) stated that the aim for the town was to restore a sense of place which was appropriate in scale and form to the architectural and historic fabric of the town, now that it had become primarily a destination, rather than a through route.

College Street roofscape looking north

5 College Street (Cedar Court)

The story of number 5 is one of immense change in size and use. The Grade II listed building was built in the late Georgian period as a three storey private house. A building is first shown on a map in 1831 and the first recorded resident was Jane Andrews in 1841, a lady of independent means with one servant. Jane lived there for at least 10 years during which time she also had a resident nurse.

Built in a large walled garden with the southern boundary hard against the Drum Stream, evidence can still be seen today in the river bank of the stone footings with the original wall above it. Within the front garden stands a Cedar of Lebanon (cedrus libani) and dated circa 1760, which means that it was planted before the house was built. No doubt, for this reason, the house was originally called "Cedar-cote," cote deriving from the Anglo-Norman word for cottage. It seems rather strange that such a fine house with gauged brick arches to sash windows and a doorway with a patterned fanlight and cornice on large brackets, would be referred to as a cottage!

The first large scale, ordnance survey map published in 1871 clearly shows the house, including a larger building along the rear elevation, which was probably stables and associated buildings as reportedly used by Mr. Boxall, an unqualified vet, for kennels during the early part of the 20th century.

No entries have been found for number 5 in the 1861, 1871 and 1881 Census but, strangely, all the heads of house that were recorded from 1841 to 1911 were female. In the census of 1891, Sophia Lusted is recorded as a woman of her own means, with a son and a daughter. The 1901 Census records Ann Prinsep living with a sister, a niece, a cook and a maid. In the 1911 Census, Louise Bowden-Smith, a widow is recorded with a nurse, a cook and a parlourmaid using the ten rooms.

In 1934 Miss Walker was in residence, followed by the only recording of a male occupant, when a Mr. McLough lived there during the mid twentieth century. Although the house was remembered as being slightly scruffy during this period, the gardens were beautiful and you had to be careful not to walk on the grass! The last recorded resident as a private house was Lady Marguerite Wilhelmine Bennett, who is known to have been living there when she died in 1963.

At some point, probably during the early 20th century, a large two-storey extension was added to the southern elevation, which regrettably stands forward and cuts into the original Georgian house, spoiling the proportions of the facade. The reason for the extension is unknown but by the early 1970s the whole building was owned by Kyle Ltd. and used as offices for their retail, decorating supplies business, a branch of which was located in Lavant Street.

In 1975 Kyle added a three storey office block across the rear and at right angles to the original building, constructed over and beyond the position of the demolished stable block. The rear garden was converted to a car park but thankfully a lovely 110 year old Atlantic Cedar (cedrus atlantica), adjacent to the southern boundary, was spared.

In 1980 Kyle were purchased by Dodge City, a fledgling, multi-outlet DIY company, who in turn, were purchased by B&Q in 1988. However, Dodge City sold the building in 1982 to Stefan Olszowski, the owner of Meon Travel who then occupied the site until 1999 when they sold the company to First Choice holidays who remained there until 2004 when they vacated the building.

The building's connection to the travel industry remained when it was purchased in 2006 by Arblaster & Clarke using part of the building as the head office of their specialist wine tour company. The remainder of the building was let out for multi-occupancy to other companies and still retains this use today.

Whilst occupied by Meon Travel, the name of the house was changed to Meon House but Arblaster and Clarke renamed it Cedar Court, a very appropriate name for a building still overshadowed by the beautiful tree that has seen so much change during the occupancy of the site.

Fairley

Built for the Leachman family in the 1870s, the impressive residence called Fairley was situated roughly where the Village now stands. The drawing – dating from about 1890 – shows the house set at an angle to the road. An attractive porch lit by windows on each side faces the curved drive to the road with an oriel widow above. At the rear, a three-storey wing opens into a conservatory and, beyond, into a two-acre garden. Along the boundary with College Street runs a flint wall with pillars flanking the entrance, while iron railings enclose the garden. It was the home of various members of the Leachman family for over 80 years.

During the half a century he spent at Fairley, Dr. Albert Warren Leachman had become one of Petersfield's foremost citizens, the Medical Officer of Health for the Urban District Council, a founder of Petersfield Cottage Hospital, chairman of the managers of Petersfield and Sheet Council schools and vicar's warden at St. Peter's Church. He was also instrumental in setting up the Working Men's Institute in Heath Road. He died in 1914 and is commemorated by an illuminated memorial tablet in the chancel of St. Peter's.

Colonel Gerard Evelyn Leachman CIE DSO

Dr. A. W. Leachman

Fairley Court

After her husband's death, his widow Louisa remained at Fairley with two of her daughters, Mildred and Janet. All three women were active in the town, performing charitable works in many different spheres of activity.

The Leachmans' youngest son, Gerard Evelyn, had an illustrious career as a political officer in the army. He reached the rank of colonel, was Petersfield's only DSO in the First World War, and was described as "another Lawrence of Arabia" for his exploits in Mesopotamia (now Iraq). He was shot there in 1920 while conducting negotiations with the Arabs and he is buried in Baghdad. He also has a plaque dedicated to him in St. Peter's Church.

Janet Leachman was the last member of the family to live at Fairley. She died in 1956 and the house became "Fairley Court", offering bed and breakfast and "excellent catering". The grand building, home to such a well-known and well-liked family, met a sad end when it was eventually demolished in the 1970s to make way for Tor Way.

The Village

The area known locally as The Village lies between College Street and Tor Way with some properties fronting onto College Street, although their address is Grenehurst Way.

The four acre site was derelict for a number of years after the demolition of Fairley Court. This area, along with George Bailey's Nurseries, part of the land owned by the United Reformed Church, The Pines, and a private house named Grenehurst, were eventually developed around a central road, Grenehurst Way.

Mrs. Gadsen, owner of Fairley Court, applied for permission to build 83 flats and garages in 1974. This was refused, along with other applications over the years. Eventually in 1984, Unit Construction applied to build 46 houses and garages and this was approved.

The terrace of three houses shown above, 60 to 64 Grenehurst Way, opposite to the entrance to Barham Road has been designed to blend into the street scene with bay windows which complement those of the three Victorian houses opposite. Number 66 to the left of the picture has part tile-hanging, and, although nearer to the street, is hidden behind hedging. The pathway to the right of the terrace provides pedestrian access to the town for the residents. To the right of this are more properties sheltered behind attractive brick and flint walls, fencing and hedging.

The old photo of College Street shows the brick

and flint wall on the right which was the boundary wall of Fairley Court. This has been preserved and the gateway shown just to the right of the street lamp is now the entrance to the pedestrian pathway leading to Grenehurst Way.

An Historic Footpath

Opposite the exit from the Central Car Park and on the north side of Cedar Court is a tarmac driveway. Seemingly of little consequence, it is in fact a public footpath, appearing on the Definitive Map last published in 2007, and will lead the pedestrian to what has been for nearly 40 years, Tor Way. But it is far more than that. The Definitive Map shows that its route not merely runs in a west-east line to Tor Way, enabling pedestrians to access Herne Farm, but, having crossed Tilmore Brook, it turns abruptly north, remaining on the west side of Tor Way but separated from it by trees and bushes; it finally leads towards Love Lane.

The path is shown in this position on the First Edition Ordnance Survey map of Petersfield published in 1871, and offered pedestrian access between the town and the Union Workhouse, as it then was, in Love Lane, immediately to the north of the then Petersfield to Midhurst branch railway.

Between College Street and Tilmore Brook, the path also gave vehicular access not only to what was Clarendon Hall (a drill hall behind the then Cedarcote) and Clarendon Yard (a series of unprepossessing workshops), but it led also to a pair of brick semi-detached cottages, numbered respectively 7 and 9 College Street. These were erected at the end of the 19th century, and have remained in residential use since then, although they have both been almost doubled in size by sympathetic two-storey extensions.

15 College Street (Northbrook)

Known nowadays by its original name of Northbrook, this property has been known as Northbrook Villa or Northbrook Cottage at various times in its 150 year history. Remarkably, the story of this house and its inhabitants encompasses many aspects of College Street generally: the links with Churcher's College, British colonial rule in India, religious non-conformism and, most recently, the forces Home from Home canteen in Petersfield during the Second World War.

The 1841 Tithe Map shows that plot 55, owned by the Jolliffe family, was pasture land, and, in 1865, Sir William George Hylton Jolliffe of Heath House, Petersfield and Mr. Charles Edwin Collins of Petersfield signed a lease concerning a small triangle of land forming part of plot 55 and fronting the turnpike road (now College Street).

Three years later, it was Collins who built the house – called it Northbrook (probably after its position in relation to the Drum Stream) – and subsequently leased it to Alfred Dusautoy, who was the Headmaster of Churcher's College from 1849 to 1877.

Digressing for a while on the next phase of Northbrook's history, we need to look at the gradual incursion of the Money family into this part of Petersfield: William Taylor Money b. 1769, the central figure in the painting (right), was the eldest of five brothers. He wears the uniform of a lieutenant of the East India Company marine service, thus associating himself with the origins of Churcher's College itself.

William married a cousin of his, Eugenia, and their fifth child, David Inglis Money was born in 1807 in Bombay, whose younger sister, Mary Eugenia, was also to be involved later in the Northbrook story. David, too, entered the service of the East India Company, married Jane Deans in 1830, and their son, Charles Leonard Money, born in 1839, was also to feature in the story of Northbrook.

David Inglis Money's career led finally to the position of Judge of the Supreme Court in Calcutta. He retired in 1860 and moved to Stodham Park, close to Petersfield, where he died in 1880. He had become the successor to Alfred Dusautoy as tenant of Northbrook Cottage and, in his will, he bequeathed the property to W. J. Money and his cousin Wigram Money (his eldest son and executor) in trust to permit his sister, now Mrs. Mary Eugenia Cameron, "to occupy the house and garden during her lifetime." On Mary Eugenia's death, the house continued to be held in trust for Charles Leonard Money.

Sadly, within a few months, Ewen Henry Cameron had died, and Mary Eugenia returned to live with her widowed mother Eugenia in Cadogan Place, Chelsea. By 1874, when her brother David Inglis Money bought the lease, we know that she was living in Northbrook Villa, where she died in 1892.

David and Jane Money's younger son, Charles Leonard Money, was an army officer. He married Cathleen Fanny Grantham in Melbourne in 1880, but the couple returned to England and, thanks to the trust set up by David's uncle, Northbrook became their home.

In the census of 1911, the family were still in Northbrook Cottage. Charles stated he was a "lieutenant retired." Cathleen Eugenia was now 12, and Agnes Mabel was 10. They had both been born in Northbrook Cottage. Two sons had died, Charles in 1905 and David in 1908. Robert and Jack were away at school, A cook and a housemaid completed the household. Charles Leonard died in 1919 at Northbrook Cottage. It was Charles' daughter Kathleen who, during the Second World War, set up the Home from Home canteen for servicemen a short walk from her childhood home in College Street.

After Charles' death, his widow Cathleen continued to live in Northbrook Cottage, but by 1930, it was decided to sell the cottage and the mortgage was paid off in preparation for the sale. After some 60 years, the Money family finally left Northbrook for good.

The house was sold to Dr. Lily Dorothea Taylor. Born in 1892 into a Non-conformist family in Leicester, her mother Mary Ellen Taylor (née Bennet) was twice imprisoned for her activities on behalf of the Women's Suffrage movement. Her brother Garth, born in 1896, was a pupil at Bedales School.

Lily Dorothea was registered as a doctor in 1916. By 1927, her address was given as 11 Chapel Street Petersfield (now Kimber Shoes) and in 1930, she bought Northbrook Villa from the trust set up by David Inglis Money.

In 1932, Dr. Catherine Jane Ormerod, aged 31, came from Yorkshire to Petersfield to join Dr. Taylor's practice and she, too, lived at Northbrook as a tenant of Dr. Taylor. In 1950, Dr. Taylor finally sold Northbrook Villa to Dr. Ormerod for the sum of £6,000.

In 1962, "Northbrook Villa" was sold to Dr. Reginald Bowesman for £7,000. Sadly, the Bowesman's son Dermot died at Northbrook in 1968 and, just three years later, Dr. Bowesman retired and he and his wife moved to 22 Chapel Street.

In the early 1970s, a great deal was changing around Northbrook. The new circulatory system, Tor Way, was being planned and the firm known as Constructions (Petersfield) Ltd. bought a small portion of Northbrook's garden from Dr. Bowesman which would, in time, become part of the housing development known as "The Village". This purchase took place in May 1971.

The following October, Dr. & Mrs. Bowesman sold Northbrook to Mr. and Mrs. Middleton Smith. It was then sold on in 1981, before being bought by its present owners in 1999.

Northbrook Villa in the 1870s

Baileys Nursery and Garden Centre

This picture, from the 1980s, with the "Baileys" advertisement board on the College Street pavement, reflects a connexion with the site that lasted more than a century, ending with the current use of the site as the southernmost part of "The Village". Examination of Ordnance Survey maps from the First Edition published in 1871 for the ensuing hundred years reveals the continuous use of no. 11 College Street and its grounds as a nursery.

In 1841, plot 54 on the Petersfield Tithe Map is described as a house and nursery. It was owned by Sir William Jolliffe and in the occupation of Richard Brewer and others. However, as Richard Brewer "occupied" many sites in College Street, it may be surmised that he held leases of them, and sublet, probably in this case to a John Eade, who is later shown in a trade directory as a seedsman. The early Victorian censuses lack any means of identifying many individual properties, but successive decennial returns may profitably be used to link people to places. So it is with the nursery site, immediately to the north of the footpath to Love Lane.

The 1851 Census also revealed in College Street, seemingly on the eastern side, the Bailey family, of whom the household head, John, was also a seedsman. The 1865 Harrods Directory refers to John as Nurseryman and Seedsman. By 1881, John, in his sixties, was living, presumably in the building seen in the photo, with his several daughters, and a 24-year-old son William. John Bailey remained at no.11 College Street until his death in 1894. William Bailey was to expand the business with the opening of a florist's shop at no.1 Chapel Street, Petersfield. The 1901 Census described him as "Florist, Gardener and Employer", living in Chapel Street with his wife Harriet, and 19-year-old son George, a Florist and Gardener's Assistant. Meanwhile, the householder of no. 11 College Street was Henry Tribe, a market gardener, with his wife and four children. Ten years later, Henry Tribe was described as a "Florist's Manager", suggestive of his employment by William. The association of Henry Tribe with the Bailey family would last for more than a generation.

The 1911 Hylton Estate sale shows that the freehold of the nursery had remained with the Jolliffe family. Whilst the census tells us that Henry Tribe was the actual occupier, the Jolliffe papers show that the headlease was in favour of a Miss Dora Groome for 21 years from 1900, paying an annual rent of £22. The buildings were described as having two bedrooms, two sitting rooms, a shop, a kitchen and a scullery. The nursery glasshouses were fixtures added by later tenants.

By 1911 George Bailey had set up his own home at 1 Chapel Street with his wife Ellen (née Bridle), and their first daughter. He was at this time still identified as an employee. His father William, still in his fifties but now widowed, had moved into 32 Barham Road. Whilst George Bailey appears as a Nurseryman at various local addresses in subsequent trade publications, Henry Tribe is quoted as a Florist in College Street. In 1948, Henry Tribe died, aged 85. Coincidentally or not, that year George Bailey (Nurseries) Ltd. was formally incorporated under the Companies Acts, whose directors were George himself and Frederick Lilleywhite. The latter was no mere business partner, having married George's younger daughter Mildred two years previously. George Bailey died in December 1956 leaving an estate of just under £20,000, but the company continued trading from the College Street site.

In 1985, substantial modifications and improvements were carried out to the garden centre, but that was merely a presage to its ultimate sale for development in 1986.

17 College Street

This architecturally intriguing and beautifully sited house is Grade II listed. The building is internally timber-framed and dates back to the early or mid-17th century, although its present appearance demonstrates that it was substantially rebuilt in brick in the Georgian period. Sadly, no tree-ring dating has taken place on it to ascertain its exact date of construction.

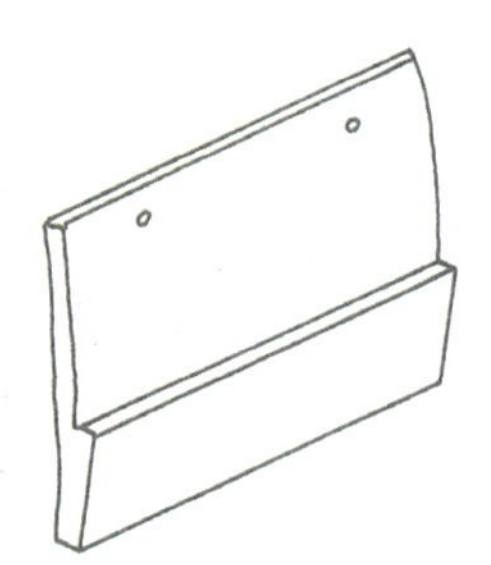

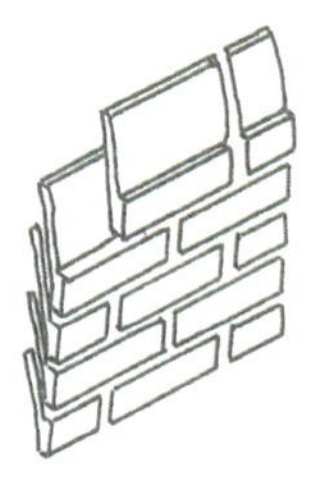

The "mathematical" tiles on the south facade (diagram above), dating back to the 18th century, were an inexpensive means of covering the original wooden frame. The overhanging tile-hung first floor, the cornice hood to the front door, and asymmetrical front facade lend the property a genuinely "olde-worlde" feel. The unfortunate subsidence to a section of the front facade only serves to accentuate this sense of ancient identity.

The interior of the house is no less puzzling: various alterations over the centuries have resulted in a hybrid, yet highly attractive architectural style. There may have been a third bay to the house, since demolished, which would account for the oddly placed beams and uncertainty about the position of the original chimney. The rear of the building reveals that a parallel two-storey range was added to the main structure at some point, probably in the 18th century, which may indicate the growing wealth of successive owners.

The whole construction does not indicate that this was a grandiose dwelling for prosperous owners. Indeed, the existence of a look-out hole in the wall between the kitchen and sitting room, together with meat hooks still visible in the front room suggest that this was a shop in Victorian times and the rear wing section was probably added to increase the space required to run a commercial business from the house.

According to the 1861 Census, the house was occupied by 39-year-old Henry Holland, a "retired" miller who had helped his father work the Steep Mill. Perhaps he had come into money from other sources shortly after his parents' deaths in the 1850s, because he had only inherited "under £300" from his father and would not have been able to purchase 17 College Street or live as a man of independent means on that amount. This apparent financial independence could also account for the alterations which he could have instigated at the property.

However, by 1891, he had taken a (much younger) new wife, Sarah, who was the daughter of a cowman living at the north end of College Street. The couple were married in London, where Henry's married sister lived but made 17 College Street their home for the next 28 years. Altogether, Henry had occupied the house for about 50 years, by which time he and Sarah had a live-in servant. When Henry died in 1916, his effects totalled almost £7,000, a considerable sum in those days. Sarah stayed at the house, now named Fir Cottage, and lived to the age of 96, dying in 1953.

19–21 College Street (Quaker Cottage)

There is evidence of a building on this site from c.1600. The surviving elements from this early dwelling are the rafters in the southern bay. In the other bays there is evidence of cross-frames with queen-strut trusses and short straight braces. The original floorboards are also still in existence, and the lack of soot on the rafters means that a chimney stack existed at this time. These features are typical of a dwelling of the early 17th century.

There is an indenture dated 1745 that states a barn plus ½ acre were purchased at this site (known in its original title deeds as "The Little Old Barn"). The barn and Colebrook Meadow were then enclosed and used as one property, presumably incorporating the original dwelling.

In 1904, there is another indenture stating that there was a dwelling house and land at no. 19, together with a large room adjoining used as a religious meeting room at no. 21. This must have been the origin of the name "Quaker Cottage" as some Non-conformist churches did operate during the Victorian era in College Street. Interestingly, Non-conformists clearly found the location of College Street suitable to their needs – perhaps sufficiently distant from the centre of town, yet within the parish boundary. There were many groups of Quakers meeting throughout Hampshire from the 17th century onwards. Petersfield Quakers met in the early days at Alton, the second oldest Meeting House in the country, and Quaker families would have gone to other towns for their meetings.

There had also been Presbyterians in Petersfield in the 17th century, the forerunners of the Congregationalists, so perhaps the nearby presence of this group in the street allowed the Quakers to feel bolstered as part of the non-conformist (the so-called Protestant Dissenters or Free Church) trend spreading across the country. Samuel Pepys, who occasionally passed through Petersfield in the 1660s on his way to Portsmouth, remarked in his Diary that he met Quakers being arrested for their faith (and the non-payment of their tithes) in various parts of the country.

By the early 20th century, however, the Society of Friends (Quaker) monthly meetings were held at the Steep home of Kenneth Barnes, a science master at Bedales School. This transferred in 1938 to Winton House in the High Street, where it became a weekly occurrence, forming part of the Alton, Southampton and Poole Monthly Meeting. In 1949, the Petersfield meeting transferred to the Dorking, Horsham and Guildford Monthly Meeting and again in 1961, when it linked to the Guildford and Godalming Monthly Meeting until 2008.

The original dwelling is covered by the two northern rooms, plus the two bedrooms above. The roof beams and the 'quartering' in the walls are still a feature to this day, together with a 'coffin hatch' in the ceiling of the sitting room to the bedroom above.

Conversions over the years have gone through several discernable stages with a second set of roof beams within the roof and rafters which supports the current slate roof. There is a bricked up window aperture on the west wall that indicates this was done to avoid the window tax [incidentally, this was introduced by William III, whose statue stands in Petersfield's Market Square – Ed.] which was levied to raise taxes from 1696 until 1851.

The house has continued to be altered since the Second World War: William Rotherham sold the cottage and some land at the rear in 1953 to build Grenehurst (1954). He was a butcher at E. J. Baker's in the High Street. His wife ran a general stores (grocer's) at no. 19, with its entry via a front door onto College Street. During the 1950s, this property incorporated a sweet shop which, naturally, was very popular with local children.

When Joan Griffiths and her husband bought Quaker Cottage from Mr. R. Hickling in 1984, they let it out to tenants for ten years. They found it haunted and smelling of fish! They then refurbished every room and the garden and lived there for six years in the 1990s. They had some difficulty getting upstairs, as the staircase was situated virtually in a cupboard.

When Cubitt and West put the property on the market in 1984, it was stated that "the property dates back to 1640, and was once divided into two cottages. Its use as a single dwelling goes back many years."

The Pines

On the 1841 Tithe Map, the site of what was to be the house known as "The Pines" formed part of a plot of pastureland owned by Charles Greetham and used by Alfred Dusautoy (master at the nearby Churcher's College) and others. The site is bounded on the west by what is now the garden of Quaker Cottage, and to the north by the terrace of four small cottages which had been built by Charles Greetham himself.

So, who lived in "The Pines" (pictured above, with the British School to the north), the brick and tile house with pine trees in the rear garden? Ann Rand (née Nockolds b. 1834) was born into a family of land agents and auctioneers which had a long connection with the town of Saffron Walden in Essex. It was their founder, Alfred Nockolds (b. 1847), who provides the vital clue linking Ann Nockolds to Petersfield: her future husband, William Rand, had also been born in Saffron Walden. William and Anne were married in 1862 and had a son, John, born in 1865. However, William died six years later and Anne was left to bring up the child on her own. It seems, therefore, that Alfred had found his widowed sister a new home in the town where he was working. By the age of 17, John was a pupil estate agent in Hertfordshire, but, at the same time, his mother was listed in the 1881 Census as living at "The Pines" in College Street, Petersfield.

Sadly, Anne became unwell and went to stay in Dulwich with her late husband's brother, Dr. John Rand, dying there in 1885, aged 51. After her death, it is possible that "The Pines" either had a short term tenant or remained empty for a time. Certainly it was unoccupied at the time of the 1891 Census. At some point after that, the (spinster) Misses Mary and Sarah Walker moved into the house, possibly after the death of their father, James, who ran Manor Farm, Buriton. Sarah died in 1913, leaving £4,000 to her sister Mary.

By the 1970s, the volume of traffic using College Street was such that plans were drawn up for a new circulatory system. This entailed the demolition of several properties, including "The Pines" which, although not needed for Tor Way, could be used for access to the new development, The Village.

"The Pines" (described in the press as "a once proud Petersfield house") became the site of garages for The Village. There exists an interesting account in the *Petersfield Post* of September 26th 1974 of the later demolition of the building. "The demolition contractor, Mr. Henry Keet, struck the first mortal blow to "The Pines" on August 30th of this year...exactly 100 years and 3 days after the foundation stone was laid. Under the foundation stone, Mr. Keet came upon a port bottle containing a 100-year-old copy of the *West Sussex Gazette* (the paper with a circulation of 29,000, the largest in the South of England at the time).

25–31 College Street

These four modest cottages, with rendered elevations under a slate roof, forming a terrace, always appear to have been in residential occupation. They are not distinguished by any bay windows on the front elevation, and have the appearance of being just one room wide, with a common chimney stack between nos. 25 and 27, and another between nos. 29 and 31. Each cottage has a frontage of no more than sixteen feet. The basic structure under a single hipped roof doubtless dates back to their construction some 180 years ago. Ordnance Survey maps of the late 19th century reveal the presence of a well in the rear garden of what would be 27 or 29, doubtless serving the occupiers of all four cottages. To provide more modern sanitary and kitchen facilities, and more living space, subsequent rear extensions have been added by their owners to each, at various stages in the latter part of the 20th century, and each cottage is now graced with a front porch. The earliest Ordnance Survey maps also show that, set back some distance from the back of the cottages, part-way down their gardens, and behind nos. 27–31, were a bank of outhouses woodhouses, or perhaps the original privies. The garden areas behind the position of these former outbuildings now offer to the current residents car parking accessed from Grenehurst Way. These originally tiny properties were very much built as workmen's cottages, as can be seen from the type of families appearing in the 1891 Census: the householders were respectively a gardener, a brewery cellarman, a builder's carman, and a coachman.

No documentary evidence has been found of any buildings on the site before the 1830s. However, in an Indenture of August 1835 , John Smith Leese and Mary Ann Leese convey to Charles Greetham their half share in a long lease of number of properties (he already owning the other half), including "all that piece or parcel of meadowland called Colebrooks and cowhouse (then) in the occupation of Alfred Dusautoy, And also those four cottages and woodhouses erected and built by the said Charles Greetham on part of the said hereditaments and premises intended to be hereby assigned with the gardens used therewith now in the occupation of Messrs. Barton, Kent, Hall and Parker." The cottages appear on the 1840 tithe map as a single unit of 20 perches (an eighth of an acre) but, interestingly, the outhouses fall into the adjacent parcel of pasture land encompassing what would become Grenehurst, and The Pines. The "owner" of both these parcels is shown as Charles Greetham, and the "occupier" was Alfred Dusautoy.

Although Charles Greetham had built the cottages, he held them under a long lease, and the freehold remained with the Jolliffe family, the Lords Hylton. Indeed, they were later to receive an acknowledgement rent from the Congregational Church for the privilege of their maintaining the windows of what was then the British School looking immediately out over no. 31, and, as we will see, the cottages formed part of the sale of Lord Hylton's Petersfield Estate in 1911.

The census of 1901 confirms that the heads of all four households were workers of some description, all born locally. James Sopp, the domestic gardener at 25, was born in Sussex, nearly 60 years previously, had already been living at the cottage for at least ten years, and also appeared in the 1911 Census. His wife was not shown as having any occupation, but their 25-year-old daughter lived with them and worked from home on her own account as a dressmaker. William Woodger, a brewery cellarman, also aged 59, had lived with his wife at no. 27 for over 20 years. By 1911, Rhoda Woodger was widowed. Number 29 housed the most people: Henry Harris, an employed brewer's drayman, aged 40 and his wife Kate, and their two children, aged 12 and 9 occupied the property. The census also reveals Frank Flipp, aged 14 a stick factory errand boy (doubtless working at the factory on the opposite side of College Street), as their son, but it might reasonably be supposed that he was the son of Kate only, who appeared elsewhere in Petersfield as a 15-year-old servant Kate Flipp in the 1881 Census. The Harris family were to remain as tenants through to the 1911 Census. Finally, at no. 31, was 46-year-old Charles Alderman, who was the coachman for Dr. Leachman of Fairley (see panel), his wife and daughter. By 1911, they had moved away.

It is in 1911 that we obtain the clearest insight into the accommodation provided in these four cottages as they form Lot 28 in the sale of "the Petersfield

Estates", sold by order of the Rt. Hon. Lord Hylton. The properties are described as a block of four freehold cottages, with extensive garden ground and having a side cartway approach (on the southern side of no. 25), to firstly a kitchen garden let to Mr. H. M. Brownfield on a yearly agreement and, further to the rear, more garden ground let on a Michaelmas tenancy to a Mr. H. Gander. It can safely be assumed that these gardens lay in two parcels of land behind the sheds. The cottages are described as being brick built, rough cast and slated, with two bedrooms, sitting room, and kitchen with wood shed and good gardens. So each cottage has two rooms downstairs, and two upstairs. Each was let at £8 per annum to Messrs. W. and R. Luker, seemingly – judging by census occupations – for the use of brewery employees.

The British School

The British and Foreign School Society supported the construction of "British Schools" by Non-conformist churches, receiving state assistance from 1833.

In 1845 or thereabouts, part of the United Reformed church site to the south of the chapel and now forming its car park, was used to construct the British School for both boys and girls. This building, a feature of the streetscape for 120 years, was not much more than 15 feet wide, and about four times as deep: in the 1850s it is described as being attended by about 180 pupils. For some 45 years it was run by Mr. John Gray Fairbairn, with children being charged a penny or so a week to attend.

In June 1864 however, an inspector reported that the infants' school was taught by monitors in a low and poorly ventilated classroom, without any gallery. After the introduction of state education, numbers declined and it finally closed in 1895.

The building then became a public hall for a number of years, before being partitioned and the larger front section let for a variety of commercial uses.

In 1905, Victor Britnell, cycle and motor agent, (who had premises opposite The Red Lion) altered the front elevation to create four eleven-foot high glass doors: subsequent occupiers included a coachbuilder and house furnishers.

The British and Foreign School Society

In the late 18th century, to offer the opportunity of education to the poorer classes, the Quaker Joseph Lancaster pioneered a method of teaching whereby one schoolmaster supervised the teaching by older children, called monitors, of the younger ones. The first school opened in Borough Road, London in 1798. Ten years later saw the formation of a society for promoting the Royal British or Lancastrian System for the Education of the Poor. In 1814 the name of the society was changed to its current form. With the development of public provision for education in the late Victorian era the role of the Society changed to the support of teacher training and wider educational projects.

The United Reformed Church

Although the church sanctuary itself dates back to 1883, an Independent Chapel for Dissenters was first erected here in 1801, and the church fellowship can trace its origins in Petersfield much earlier. A mid-nineteenth century town history records that the church was built on the site of a former workhouse, but subsequent investigation proves this to be incorrect. The title deeds to the church site can be traced back to a lease of one thousand years granted on 2nd June 1745 by John Jolliffe to Hannah Eades, the widow of Charles Eades, the first Master of Churcher's College, from which a sub-lease was created to church trustees in 1801. The site has remained unchanged in its dimensions, save that in 1983 a triangle of land at the easternmost extremity was sold to facilitate the construction of Grenehurst Way, and "the Village" estate, facilitating the current rear access to the church garden.

An Independent Chapel had first been built in Petersfield in 1722. The Surman Index of Congregational Ministers suggests earlier ministry in Petersfield from 1690. However, by the end of the 18th century the fellowship was far from thriving, and apparently operating from premises in Cow Legs Lane, (now Station Road). It took the evangelical initiative of the London Itinerancy Society (the Village Itinerancy Association), from Hackney, Middlesex, who first brought Richard Densham to Petersfield in 1797 to invigorate the Independents in the Petersfield area. His was a hectic life, often preaching several times a day to huge crowds, at one point preaching 53 times in 25 days. He met much opposition too. On August 2nd 1800, preaching at Petersfield, Harting, East Meon, and finally to some 500 people in the street at Rogate, he was pelted with rotten eggs. Sixteen days later, he was stoned out of Alresford.

The chapel that was opened for worship on 27th September 1801 is depicted in an ancient print (below): its dimensions were thirty five feet square, with an adjoining vestry room. Galleries were added later. Richard Densham sadly was killed when flung from a gig whilst riding into Haslemere on 25th July 1803. A tablet to his memory sits above the organ in the present day church, hidden by the organ pipes.

Behind the 1801 chapel lay a graveyard, disused by the 1860s. By 1899, it was described as a "pathetic spot". One hundred and fifty years after closure, it now forms part of an attractive church garden.

The 1801 chapel itself became unsuitable for the needs of the thriving fellowship, and the congregation resolved in 1877 to replace it. By July 1881, the church had sufficient funds to carry out the scheme. In September 1882, Trustees gave permission to demolish the chapel and re-build it at an eventual cost of approximately £2000. Plans of the projected building, designed by J. B. Surman, were criticised for the sloping floor. The Building Committee and congregation felt they knew better, and to this day the slope remains. Whilst building works took place, the fellowship worshipped in the Corn Exchange, in the Square. The memorial stone to the new Chapel, under which is set a time capsule, was laid on 2nd

August 1883 by Joseph Soames and is still faintly visible on the front elevation. The chapel opened for worship on 18th January 1884.

The passer-by at the end of the nineteenth century would doubtless have used the pavement on the east side of College Street, as there was none on the west side. Whilst the front wall of the British School abutted the pavement, the church itself sat behind a dwarf wall with railings. Surman's Gothic chapel, in stone, remains today. The basic sanctuary measures approximately nine metres wide by eighteen deep. Late 20th century modifications removed the rear pews, enlarging and lightening the vestibule area behind the entrance doors. Although some interior furnishings from the Edward Barnsley workshop in Froxfield are noteworthy, the building itself was once described in Pevsner and Lloyd's Buildings of England, as "Gothic and unfortunate". Perhaps this criticism was based on the dark and uninviting red brick church hall, with its rear flat-roofed extension.

Petersfield Congregational Church, as it then was, celebrated its 250th anniversary in 1972. With the formation of the United Reformed Church nationally that year, it became pastorally linked with the smaller former Presbyterian Church of St. Paul's at Hill Brow.

During the pastorate of Revd. Peter Norris the most extensive changes to the buildings on the site have taken place. In 2007, the Victorian church hall and 1960s extension were demolished, and replaced by the modern Church Family Centre, the western elevation faced in stone, comprising reception area and hall, divided with folding screens, meeting room, minister's office, kitchen and toilets, to the design of Allen Associates Architects Ltd. of Bracknell. Costing some £663,000 to construct and equip, it was formally opened at the end of March 2008.

The Church frontage appears much as it did a century ago, save that the railings have long gone and modern glass doors have replaced the former wooden ones. Where the British School formerly stood is the access to the Church Family Centre, and a small car parking area. This is bounded on the south by a metre-high flint wall, separating the church from number 31 College Street, and is probably the lower section of the southern wall of the sometime British School. On its northern boundary, the church is separated from Churcher's Old College by an ancient two-metre-high flint wall extending to the back of the new Family Centre.

Interior of the United Reformed Church with furniture from the Edward Barnsley Workshop

Churcher's Old College

Richard Churcher, a wealthy apothecary of Petersfield, left in his will of 1722 sufficient money to provide free schooling for "ten or twelve boys" in the town "for the furtherance of their naval service" in the employ of the East India Company. His acquaintance with, and knowledge of, the East India Company stemmed from his employment with the company over many years; after retirement, he had chosen to settle in Petersfield to be near to his brother Adam, a pewterer. Richard had amassed a fortune in business and Petersfield boys were to be the lucky recipients of his generosity. In fact, the stipulation of a free education was not enforced after 1754, but the £3,000 legacy had been sufficient to buy the land, build the school, pay the salary of the "Schoolmaster" and give education, clothing and board to the scholars.

This original Churcher's College is the fine Georgian building we see at the north end of College Street today, with its main staircase still intact, its Flemish bond brickwork, sash windows at the front and casements at the rear.

Richard Churcher
(Reproduced by permission of Churcher's College)

The typically Georgian cube-shaped building had cellars dug out below it – probably to house the kitchens and servants' quarters – and these are today subject to occasional flooding. The interior of the cube was well designed, with the rooms on all floors facing either east or west, with a central passageway from north to south (in line with College Street itself). The dominant feature is the central staircase with its original oak panelling and balustrade.

The building, on a site known as Tawkes Mead, had been completed in 1729 and took in its first ten pupils in 1730 under its Master, Charles Eade, unusually for the time a layman, and whose salary amounted to £40 per annum. To provide a play area, the meadow at the rear of the building was bought, extending to the Tilmore Brook, and walled in; this wall is still partly visible. The present extension on the north side dates from the later 19th century. The south side extension is more interesting: it dates from 1762 when it was a classroom used by private pupils taken in by the Master to supplement his income. This arrangement was made to suit the Master, who had found that he was unable to live on his salary and who had negotiated the extra space with the Trustees. In fact, this space was eventually used by all pupils and their dormitories were built above this schoolroom.

The conditions of the Founder's will, which specified a syllabus primarily based around mathematics and navigation, were abandoned after a Parliament Act of 1744 and boys were no longer required to become naval apprentices, nor to board at the school. In the 18th century, most old Churcherians became tradesmen or artisans, thereby fulfilling an economic need of the town.

View along Station Road from the top of Churcher's Old College

Although some pupils were housed in the school as boarders, there were also some of the school's Trustees resident there and, in the early 18th century, a handful of girls were also educated at Churcher's. So it became a home for all its inmates and the large schoolroom served not only for classes, but also as a recreation area and as an evening bathroom, with baths brought in from the kitchen for washing in. In the mornings, according to a pupil's account of 1864, washing took place in a rudimentary construction outside the back door of the schoolroom. The engraved name of "I. Jacob" can still be seen in the brickwork of the wall where the washing queue must have formed.

Since College Street formed part of the main London to Portsmouth road at this time, it is entirely possible that both Wellington and Nelson passed by the College, the latter on his final journey to Portsmouth to embark on HMS *Victory* in 1805 in preparation for the Battle of Trafalgar.

The 19th century encompassed the reign of two members of the Dusautoy family, George and Alfred, father and son, from 1815 to 1876. Early in this period, there occurred the extraordinary case in Chancery, amply recounted in J. H. Smith's 1936 history, of maladministration by the school's charity, resulting in the College having to pay many thousands of pounds in tax to the government. In the mid-nineteenth century, the number of schoolchildren (aged between 6 and 14 years) had reached 100, but this soon dwindled, academic standards fell, the building had become cold and insanitary, the floors were worm-eaten and, in June 1877, the College closed. Its successor opened on Ramshill in 1881.

Engraving on college wall

Subsequently, the Old College building was first sold in 1877 to Lord Hylton, a governor of the College, then it passed to Dr. H. M. Brownfield in 1907, the Medical Officer of Health for Petersfield, who remained there with his family, including his son (the later Admiral Brownfield), until the late 1920s. In 1888, Dr. Brownfield had become a junior partner in the practice of Dr. Albert Leachman, who lived at

Fairley, a large detached residence also in College Street.

From 1927 until 1936, a Miss Ethel Agnes Adams took on the lease of the Old College and turned it into a boarding house or private hotel. It was then bought by the Petersfield Rural District Council who ran it as local government offices. During the Second World War, the old Georgian and Victorian schoolroom was again used as a classroom by evacuees from Battersea County School and, after the war, as a dance hall and a council chamber.

With the Local Government re-organisation of 1974, the Old College building became the property of the East Hampshire District Council. This ownership was transferred again in 1987, when the Hampshire County Council bought the building to

house the Rates Office, the Highways Department (Petersfield section), the Area Surveyor, and the Register Office for Births, Deaths and Marriages for Petersfield, with facilities for marriage ceremonies. The building, identified as a Grade II listed building, closed in 2011.

In 2014, the whole building reverted to a private family residence, with some commercial leasing on the premises, and has been extensively and sympathetically renovated and refurbished both internally and externally.

Telephone Box

At the northern end of College Street are a cluster of historic structures that enjoy Grade II Listed Buildings status: The Old College, numbers 36 and 36A, number 48, and numbers 50 and 52, as well as The Good Intent. There is also, however, an iconic item of street furniture sharing the same listed status since 1990, namely the red telephone kiosk, situated on the pavement by Petersfield United Reformed Church.

This is a K6 type telephone box, originally designed by Sir Giles Gilbert Scott (1880-1960) for the Jubilee of King George V in 1935, but not introduced until 1936. It was made by the Lion Foundry Co. Ltd. of Kirkintilloch, near Glasgow, from cast iron with a domed roof and the unperforated crowns of King George VI (1936-1952) adorning the top panels. The K6 stands eight foot four inches high, is formed of eighteen pre-cast sections, and held together by exactly two hundred screws. Each side panel and the door contain twenty-four glazed panels. The door is in fact made of teak, and the entire structure weighs about 750 kg.

About 70,000 telephone boxes of this type were originally installed nationally until production ceased in 1968, and some 2,000 of those remaining have listed status. The telephone equipment was removed from the College Street kiosk some years ago, but, unlike some 1,500 elsewhere inspirationally converted into other community uses, such as defibrillator kiosks, libraries, exhibition or information centres (as the similar but unlisted box outside the Village Hall in Steep), the box in College Street remains empty, unilluminated, and in need of repainting and the replacement of some of its glazing panels. It serves merely to shelter passers-by from adverse weather, enabling them to make their mobile calls in the dry.

Stawell Map: Petersfield 1793

Ordnance Survey Map: Petersfield 1871

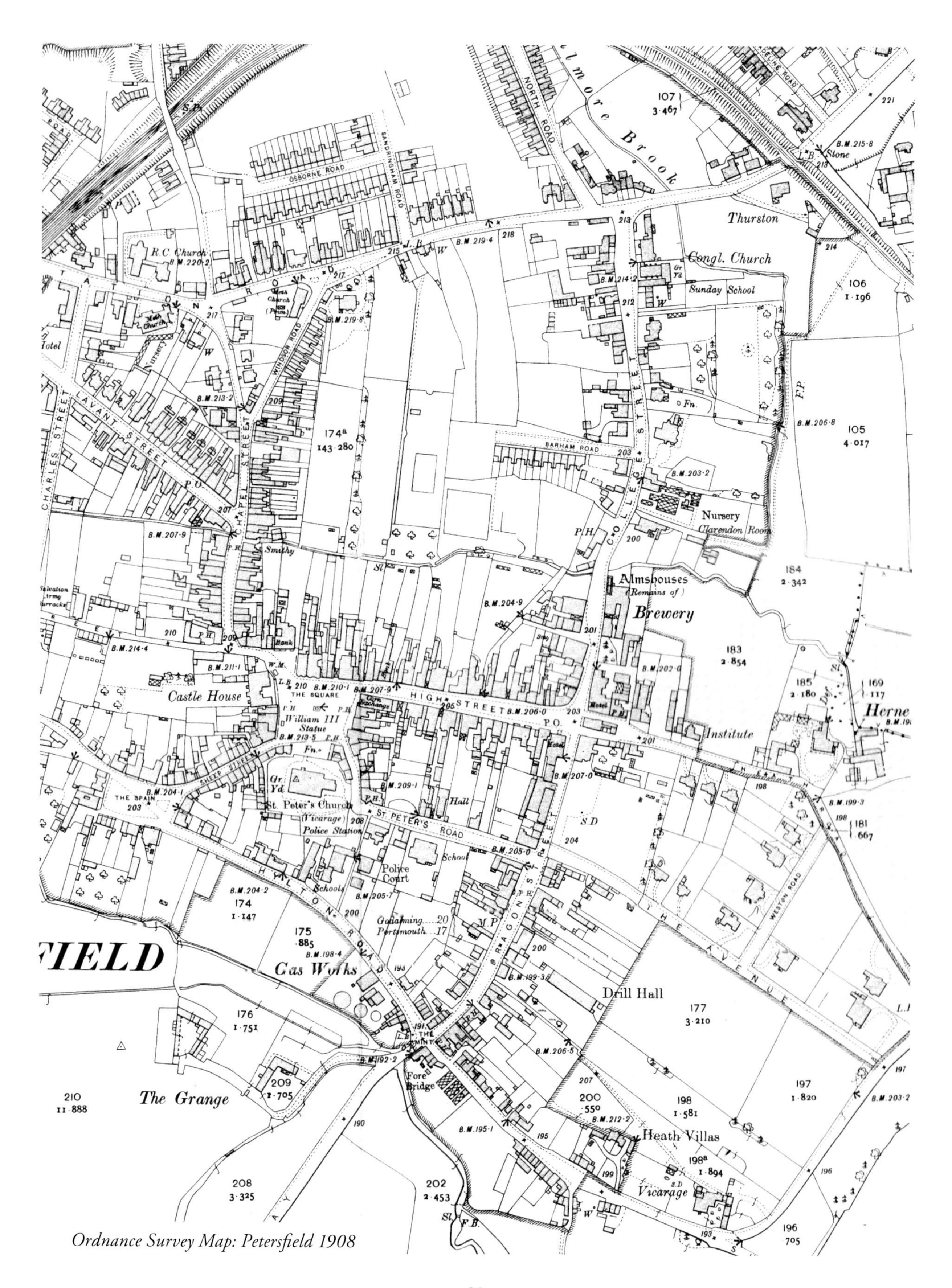

Ordnance Survey Map: Petersfield 1908

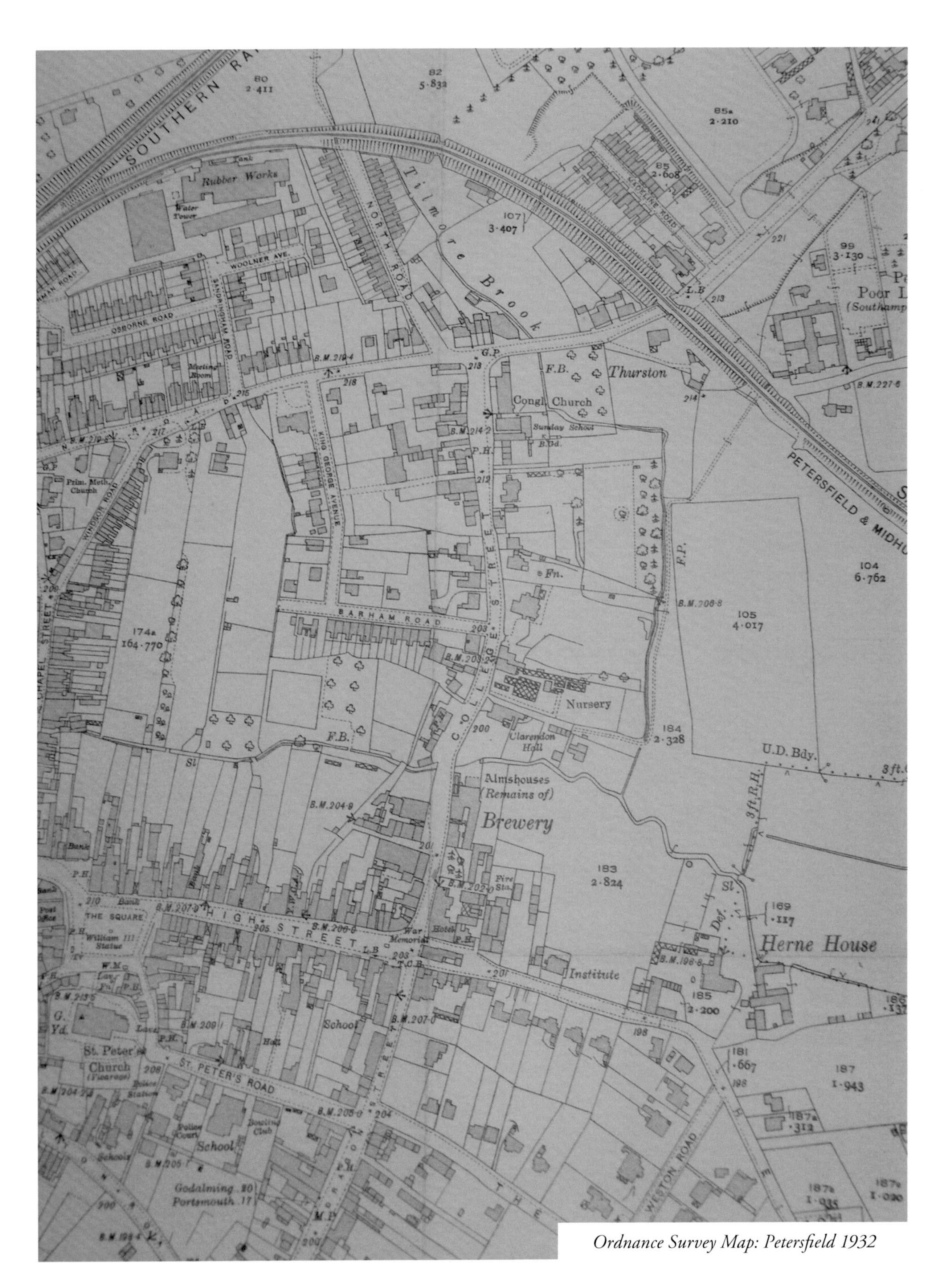

Ordnance Survey Map: Petersfield 1932

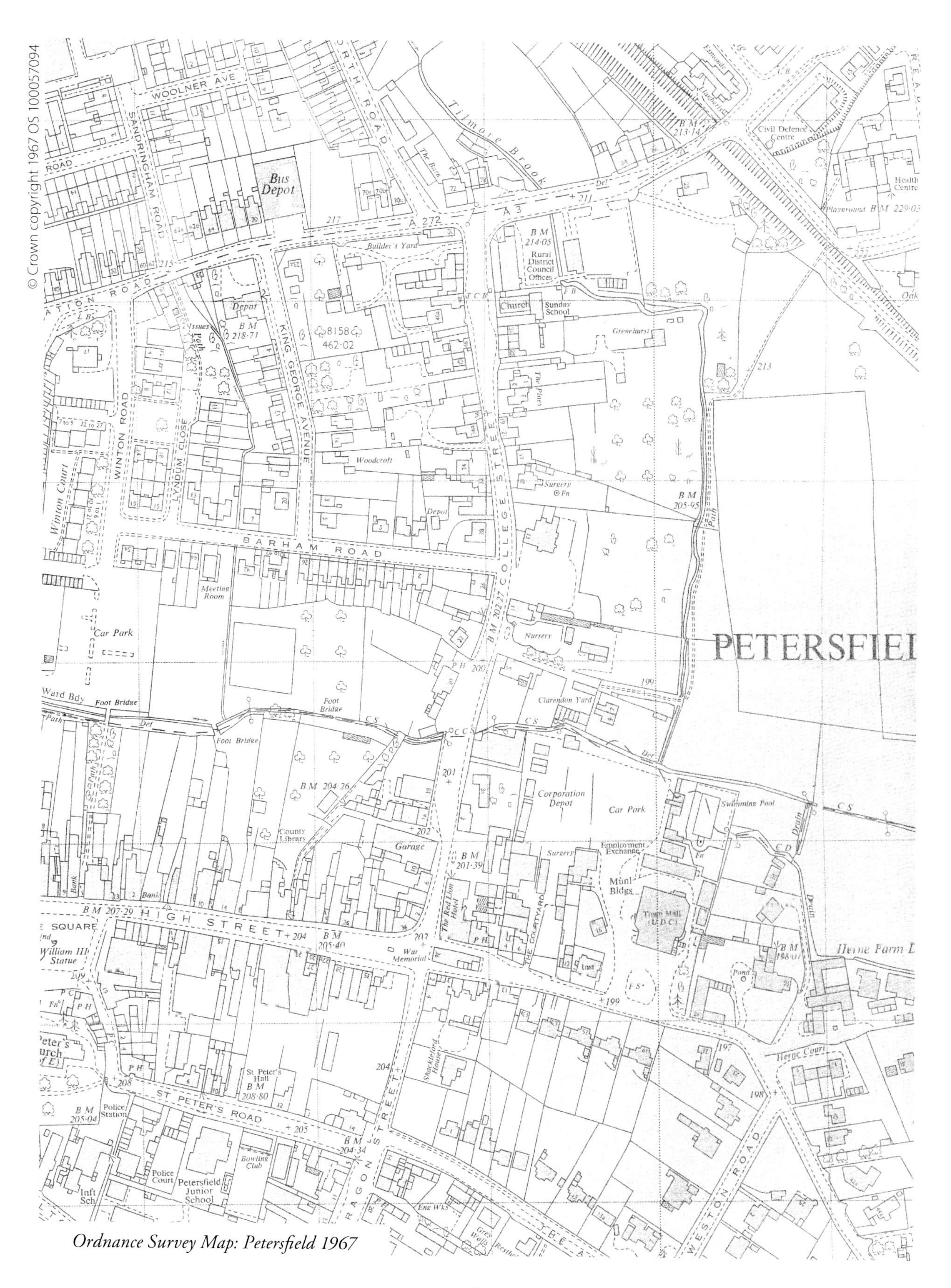

Ordnance Survey Map: Petersfield 1967

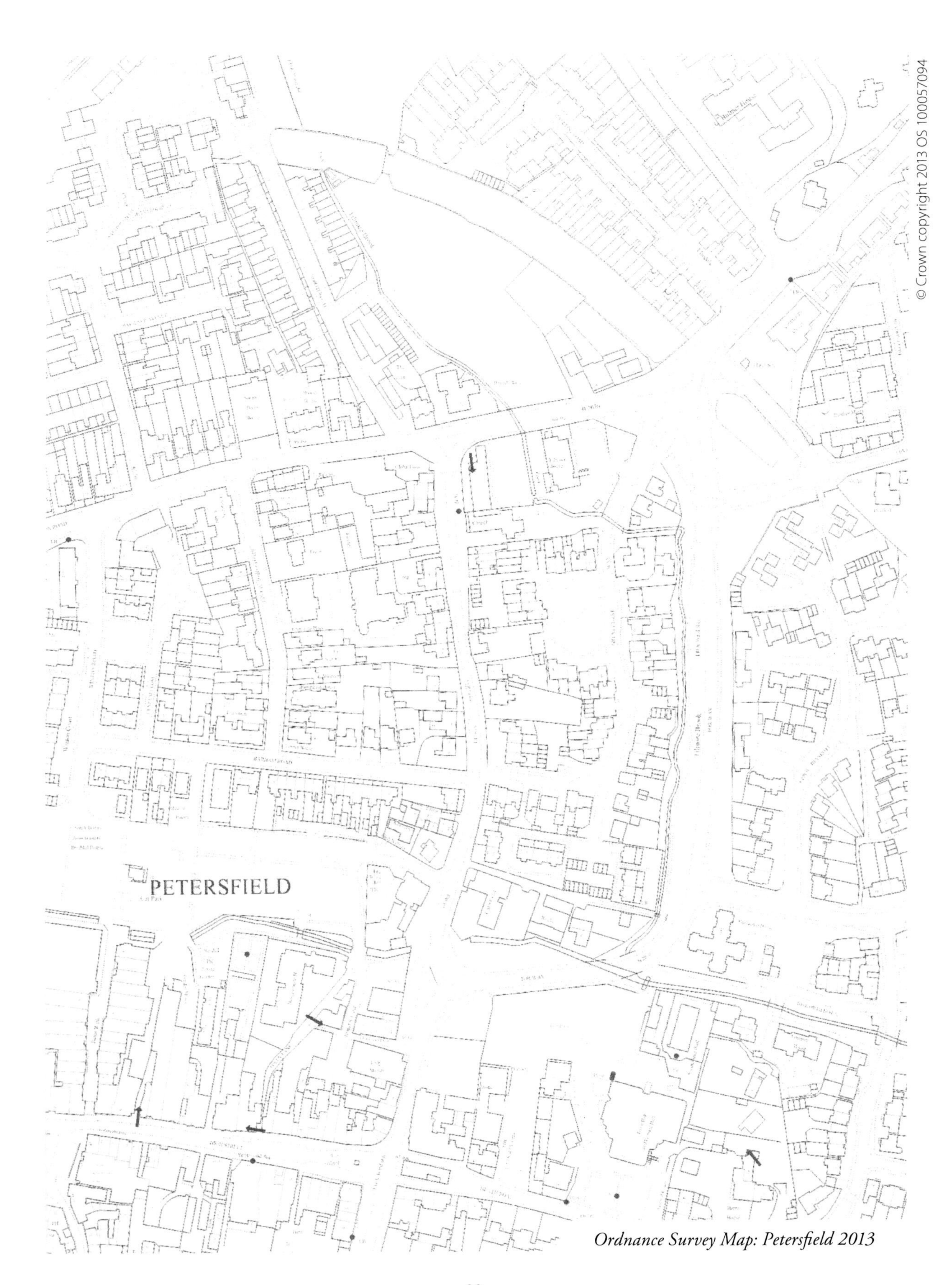

Ordnance Survey Map: Petersfield 2013

2 College Street

On the 1773 map of Petersfield, a group of four buildings are shown at the southern end of College Street, situated on the west side, opposite the Red Lion Inn. These are the properties now numbered 2, 4, 6 and 8 College Street. There is clearly a gap in the frontage between the first of these (number 2) and the nearest High Street property.

By the 1841 Census, number 2 housed a surgeon, Moses Piercey, a Portsmouth born man, together with another man, possibly a colleague, and an apprentice and two servants. Pigot's Directory of 1844 shows that he was still resident there and had married Ann Wills Fletcher. They moved to Portsmouth later in the 1840s and started a family.

In the 1850s, the property was occupied by an elderly widow of independent means, Mrs. Ann Ball, who had moved there from Ramshill and was clearly being looked after by one of her three daughters, Ann Winkworth. Mrs. Ball died in 1863 at the age of 84 and her – by now widowed – daughter moved to 20 Station Road, Petersfield.

It was at this point that the Pierson family took over the house: James Pierson was a tailor as was his older son Charles, and Mrs. Frances Pierson kept house for them and their younger son Walter, a boot and shoe shopkeeper and his wife Elizabeth who had married in 1881. The young couple eventually had three children, but the family's history was tragic: their first son died in infancy and, in 1887, Walter himself died, aged only 32. His mother had also died two years previously and James died in 1890, leaving Elizabeth with two surviving children and her husband's legacy (of £684) to run the boot and shoe shop started by Walter in his father's tailor's shop.

Elizabeth battled on for nearly 30 years and died in 1919, by which time a new house had been constructed between no. 2 College Street and the nearest High Street premises on the corner. She would undoubtedly have been content to see their shop re-occupied as a shoe shop ("Mimosa") in the early 21st century.

The later 20th century history of number 2 shows that the then resident, Caroline Hughes, married Victor Jenner of Dragon Street in 1923 and they were the founders of Jenner and Hughes, also shoe-sellers! Later occupiers of the premises included a confectioner, a hairdresser and, in the 1990s, a car parts and accessories dealer, Mr. D. Chase.

The rear view of nos. 2, 4, and 6 College Street reveal their 18th century origins

4 College Street

In 1973, the properties currently numbered 4, 6 and 8 College Street – although clearly originally one construction unit – received Grade 2 listing. Interestingly, no. 4 is the only property in College Street occupied by members of the same family for over 160 years. The family in question was the Bradleys. In the 18th century, neither no. 2 nor no. 4 belonged to the Jolliffe estate, although nos. 6 and 8 did and are therefore shown on the Jolliffe property map of 1773.

By the early 19th century, we can trace a link between the Bradleys and this property: the first, Bridger Bradley, had married Elizabeth Wheatfill and they had two sons, Bridger (Jnr.) and Henry. The older boy, born in 1803, became a tailor and was listed in Pigot's (National Commercial) Directory for College Street in 1830. He married Elizabeth Denyer in 1833 and was one of many "dissenters" of the Independent Chapel in College Street which had been built at the north end of the street in 1801. Its congregation numbered many College Street residents, including the Outridge, Eades, Bone, Vick, Todman and Gammon families, thus emphasising College Street's role in providing an alternative for people's spiritual needs to the Church of England.

Bridger Bradley's younger brother Henry married and also settled in College Street, as a shoemaker, in 1833. Their father died in 1839 and, soon afterwards, Bridger was listed as a grocer in the 1841 Census, living with his wife and two small children. Meanwhile, Bridger had moved from College Street to Cowlegs Lane (now Station Road). Sadly, he was admitted to the Petersfield Union Lunatic Asylum (in Ramshill) in 1865, with "domestic trouble" and "fear of poverty" stated as contributory factors in his demise.

Early Victorian maps of Petersfield show a Post Office at no. 4 College Street and, in the 1851 Census, Richard Eames brother of the clockmaker Henry, is shown as a Distributor of Stamps living at the southern end of College Street. By the next decennial census, however, he has changed his occupation and by then the Minchin family is running the Post Office in the High Street.

In 1861, Catherine Minchin appears in the High Street as Postmistress, Bookseller and Stationer, but the 1st edition Ordnance Survey map finally published in 1871 continues to mark what is now no. 4 College Street as a Post Office. (It may therefore be that she lived in the High Street but rented part of no. 4 as a trade premises).

She was the last of the Minchins in Petersfield, a family which had lived here since the mid-18th century. The use of 4 College Street as a Post Office was relatively short-lived, however, and, in 1870, the Post Office moved back to the High Street, in what is now Rowswells.

Henry Bradley and his wife Martha were resident with their son William – a watchmaker – at no.

4 in the 1870s. William and his wife Louisa sadly lost four of their six children shortly after they were born, but their sons Wilfred and Llewellyn started their own business in Lavant Street at the turn of the century (picture right). Wilfred was, like his father, a watchmaker, while his brother became a stationer. The name of Bradley still (just) survives on the rear wall of the business at the corner of Lavant Street and Chapel Street (now Sue Ryder charity shop).

William and Martha remained in the house; Martha died in 1909 and William in 1916, but the house in College Street was kept in the family's possession until very recently. It was a business selling second-hand woodworking tools, an antiques market, a women's clothes shop and then, in the 1990s, Bretts Wool Centre, run by Graham Brett and Sally Howell.

After refurbishment in 2014, the old shop is now a business premises.

Needlecraft shop retains thread of town history

By BRIAN MUSTOE

A Petersfield needlecraft shop is a reminder of earlier times.

Visitors to Bretts Needlecraft Centre, at 4 College Street, get swept up in the atmosphere of a romantic age. It is possible for them to sense the craftsmen who must have toiled with their hands to create the intriguing building.

A trip from the cellar to the attic is an explorer's dream adventure – you are not quite sure what to find through the next door, around the next corner or up the next stair.

Mind the step down from the pavement as you enter into the shop and cast a glance to the right, where you will spot an ancient elm surround fireplace, enhanced by the displays of needlework.

Pass through to the middle showroom, look down and you see the bare flagstone floors laid more than 300 years ago; look up, and you notice the original ceiling beams.

Staircases twist up to other floors, passing internal windows, nooks and crannies, and as long as you mind your head and remember to duck you can enter other fascinating rooms without a straight line in sight.

You can feel the floor sloping away from your feet as every room has an appealing lopsided look.

The building, opposite the Red Lion, was built more than 300 years ago.

It was acquired by the Bradley family in the 1870s.

They ran it as a jewellers until about 1916, when the business transferred to Lavant Street.

The property remained the property of the family – although many other people have traded from there subsequently.

In recent years these have included a business selling second-hand woodworking tools, an antiques market and women's clothes shop.

The present occupiers are Brett Howell Associates, principally chartered accountants, although partner Sally Howell's initial needlecraft hobby is steadily acquiring more and more of her business time.

Although she had her eye on the shop a couple of years ago, the needlecraft business began in St Peter's Road.

It moved to College Street in October, becoming Bretts Wool Centre.

The building lends itself to the needlecraft business, and they have done the absolute minimum to alter it – apart from some fresh wall decoration and removing several layers of covering from those flag stones.

The business has a national reputation, with one customer coming once a fortnight from Stratford upon Avon, and is arranging to cater for coach parties.

It operates a full-time mail-order service and has plans in the new year to include a teaching class for The Learning Curve.

Sally believes the present revival in needlecraft is because so many modern things are plastic and disposable and it is nice to keep something natural.

It is very easy, with guides to get started – and once you are away you are hooked, she says.

Contemporary cross-stitch designs show the appeal across the age-range, and Sally says they also have some very talented men who are good customers.

● The adults in the picture are the grandparents of the pr owner Eric Bradley. The picture was take either to mar golden jubilee of Queen Victoria in 1887 or the diamond j in 1897.

● Bringing history up to the present day, partners Graham Brett and Sally Howell, outside their new shop in College Street.

College Street in 1851

The 1851 Census offers a snapshot of Petersfield just before the arrival of the railway. Sadly, particular properties can rarely be identified with certainty, as house names are absent and street numbering did not then exist. Census enumerators operated no set pattern on their rounds, often criss-crossing streets.

The general direction of the survey is revealed by the first entry, Robert Crafts, The Red Lion Innkeeper, and last, Alfred Dusautoy, Master of Churcher's College, with its 13 scholars aged 9-13, all locally born bar one. There were two uninhabited and 36 inhabited properties. Four of these were the almshouses, households headed by paupers, the blind single woman Hannah Tomlins, two married couples and a widow and her dressmaker daughter. Apart from Robert Crafts, with five servants, some probably his hotel staff, and five visitors, there is another innkeeper, the widow Frances Wade, doubtless at the old White Hart, where there were six lodgers. There were also two other beer sellers, or maltsters.

There are three householders listed as boot and shoemakers, one of whom, Henry Chapman also housed a journeyman bootmaker and an apprentice whilst there is one general dealer, William Chase, accommodating a shopman and two porters, perhaps his living-in shop assistants. The census shows one other merchant, an ironmonger, a watch and clockmaker, a baker, a grocer and a tailor.

There were two craftsmen householders who were employers in their own right; a stonemason employing five men, and a bricklayer employing three. There were three gardeners or seedsmen, one blacksmith, a carter, a postman and four labourers. Five householders gave no occupation, or were of independent means, proprietors of houses, or annuitants. Although we find twenty servants living-in, only six of these might be regarded as domestic servants in private houses, a further two being nurses.

Excluding the ten visitors, there were 173 residents in College Street on Census night. The average age of householders was 49, the age spread being from 27 to 84. One third of the householders were Petersfield born, and another third within a radius of some ten miles. Twenty households comprised married couples, and thirteen of the wives were born within ten miles of the town. Seven householders had not been married; there were six widows and three widower householders.

The 36 properties in College Street are unlikely to offer a full cross-section of a market town, but craft, retail, hospitality and building trades all appear. The chief surprise is the lack of direct reference to agriculture, perhaps as the term "labourer" included some farm workers.

6–8 College Street

Unlike their neighbours, 6 and 8 College Street were two of the properties owned by Sir William Jolliffe in the Borough of Petersfield and, as such, carried votes for him in parliamentary elections. The Jolliffe property map of 1773 indicates that the northern section (today, no. 8) was marginally larger than no. 6, extending further back from the street.

Pigot's Directory and census returns of the early 19th century suggest that the two sections were in fact used as one unit. The first recorded family to have lived there were the Todmans: David was a blacksmith and he and two of his two sons (David and his wife Mary had eleven children altogether) were all listed as ironmongers. However, the family may well have been there much earlier as the younger children were baptised in the Dissenters Chapel (see under United Reformed Church) from 1812 onwards.

Both parents died in their sixties in the 1840s, but the two eldest children remained in College Street, John continuing his father's profession for a further 20 years, with his sister, Mary Ann, working as his housekeeper. They both died in 1866.

Another blacksmith, George Pond, moved into the property soon afterwards, so we might assume that the smithy was at the rear of the premises, possibly occupying part of the garden behind no. 8 or no. 10 and therefore accessible (for coach horses using the Turnpike) from what is now Crawter's Lane. From this point onwards, the two properties were separate units, with the Ponds – and two lodgers - in one section and a new couple, William Joy and his wife in the other.

William Joy was an ex-sergeant instructor in the School of Musketry at Hyde in Kent. He had moved with his first wife Sarah Jane to Petersfield some time between 1871 and 1874. In that year his wife died and, in 1876, he married Martha Bradley from neighbouring no. 4. We know that William Joy was running a stationer's and hairdresser's somewhere in College Street by an entry in White's Directory of 1878.

The Ponds moved further up College Street (this would appear to be a common feature of College Street residents, as a mark of social progression) in the 1880s and, by the 1890s, yet another blacksmith, Edwin Hood, had moved into no. 8 with his wife Caroline and their family.

Both William and Martha Joy died in the first decade of the 20th century and the two family homes now reverted to one single unit. Until 1921, the building housed produce for the Petersfield Women's Institute, located on the nearby corner of the High Street (below). From the 1920s until the start of the Second World War, the 6-8 College Street unit was transformed into a "music warehouse", serving the needs of Percy Whitehead's large "Music Studio" which took over from the Institute. At the same time, Miss Thirza Street, a confectioner and spinster, lived in the College Street premises and remained there until her death in 1947.

Since the Second World War, 6-8 College Street has regrettably seen its original features destroyed and its facade and interior reflect a "modern" office premises like many others in Petersfield.

10–12 College Street (The Folly)

An examination of the 1773 map of the Jolliffe properties in the town shows that this whole site was known as White Hart Garden – probably indicating that it was being used by visitors to the (adjoining) White Hart inn on the High Street. By 1842, however, the Tithe Map shows buildings occupying the site, so the original premises must date from the late 18th or early 19th century. It is possible that these buildings were constructed at about the same time as John Cross's new White Hart inn of 1808 close by on the College Street turnpike and which backed onto the old White Hart inn at nos. 18-20 High Street.

In the censuses of the Victorian era, the site was identified as "shops"; however, a smithy at the rear of the premises which afforded access via what is now Crawter's Lane may indicate that several families of blacksmiths named Todman were living here with their families at least between 1841 and 1861, followed by the Pond families between 1871 and 1881, followed again by the Hood family in 1891. The nature of their trade may have suggested a suitable premises for a cycle repairer, Sidney Frank, to take over the property shortly afterwards.

No. 10 then became the location of the College Street Cycle Works under the proprietorship of Britnell and Bramley, who carried out cycle repairs and were agents for Humber Cycles.

By 1907, Victor Britnell, the businessman-owner had realised that motor vehicles were the way forward and, with Thomas Crawter, an electrical specialist, they formed Britnell and Crawter Ltd., Cycle and Motor Agents and Makers. However, to accommodate their new business they decided to demolish the existing premises and build a new garage and workshop. The construction of this building caused considerable controversy as council permission had not been sought.

Demolition of the existing building had commenced before requested plans were submitted and the council only agreed to the new building subject to it being moved back four feet. This was the narrowest point on College Street and the county council had requested that it should be widened.

College Street Cycle Works, which stood on the site of the present Folly Market. (Petersfield Museum)

Britnell and Crawter did not initially accept this proposal but, after complex legal advice, they agreed to comply so long as they were paid £100 for the strip of land. Construction was then completed with this imposing building looking externally much as it does today, with the step back from the adjoining building still clearly visible.

Workshop and showrooms were on the ground floor with petrol pumps located close to the building on the forecourt, where today tables and chairs are placed in the warmer months. The offices and stores were on the first floor, where the restaurant is now situated. During the First World War, a Red Cross ambulance was kept in the garage, with Mr. Britnell being one of its drivers, when required. After the war, the Folly Market space was a garage for Southdown buses, before they transferred to a new garage in Station Road (now U2 Tyres).

As motoring pioneers in the town, Britnell and Crawter had stopped dealing in cycles by the early 1920s. Business grew with the rise in popularity of the motor car and they prospered in the following decades.

There is no evidence of them making motor cars, as their original title suggested, but they became agents for many of the well known British manufacturers including Austin, Morris, Riley, Daimler, Humber, Lanchester and Rolls Royce. They also sold motorised mowers from Atco and Dennis, tractors from Fordson and even de Havilland Moth and Cirrus aircraft. If this wasn't enough, they also offered flying tuition!

By the early 1930s they had outgrown the premises and additional facilities were built on Station Road opposite College Street – where Britnell House is today. Both partners retired shortly before the Second World War and the business was sold in the mid-1950s to the Wadham Stringer Group. They retained the building until the mid-seventies when a new workshop and showrooms were built in King George Avenue with frontage on to College Street – where Cremorne Place now stands.

No. 10 College Street was then sold starting a new life as The Folly Market and Antiques Centre in 1978. It had eight shops on the ground floor selling an array of high quality antiques including, furniture, jewellery, porcelain and costume. The Folly Wine Bar opened a year later on the first floor. Interestingly, you can still see, on the roof timbers of the bar, the locations for exhaust pipes stored there when it was a garage, which adds a fascinating link to the building's past.

Over the following years the format of this multi-use building has gradually changed. Whilst The Folly Wine Bar remained, in 1997 Jerry Hicks opened The Folly Wine and Ale House on the ground floor, which today is known as The Folly Bar Downstairs.

The Folly Market still thrives as an important and a unique trading area within the town, now with fewer antique shops but a good selection of different retailers and food outlets.

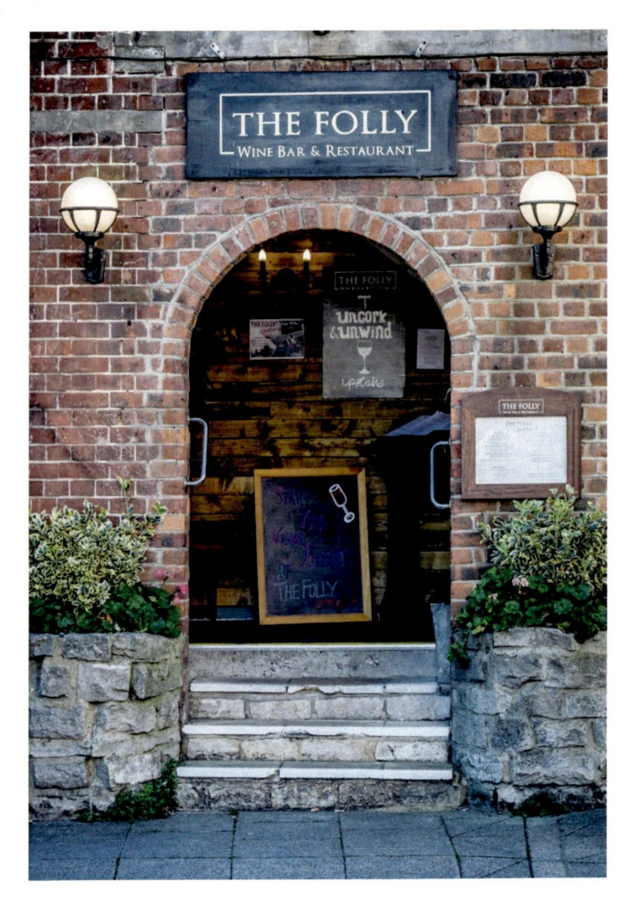

Crawter's Lane

Leading off College Street, Crawter's Lane is shown in green on the plan above in the 1900s, and the buildings have not changed much in the intervening years. For the origin of the name, see the chapter on the Folly (10-12 College Street). We know that these small properties were built between 1840 and 1870 and were probably used as small shops or workshops as the town grew.

Britnell and Crawter's Garage and car showroom occupied the building which is now the Folly Wine Bar, and the Folly Market was used as their workshops. This building was extended at some time, possibly in the 1930s, and a boiler room and oil store was built on the back.

On the other side of the lane, the building fronting College Street and which now houses Petaprint was a hairdresser's in the 1950s. At this time, the building immediately behind it was the Punch and Judy bakery and, upstairs, Mr. Hellyer, a tallyman, plied his trade selling furniture and mattresses.

The next building was occupied by the Red Cross office and both of these buildings are now used as offices. Following these, as we proceed up the lane, Bill Wiggins used the front of the premises as a garage and, behind this, Hall, Pain and Foster had a store for items used when they held an auction. This is now a hair salon.

16–18 College Street

A 1773 map shows the site on which this late Georgian building now stands as vacant land. The first known occupant was in 1830 when John Chase was recorded in the National and Commercial Directory as being a grocer and tea dealer, corn dealer and tallow chandler.

This substantial property had twelve rooms and was connected by a room width upper floor, over a gateway, to the building next door (now number 16), which was part of the overall property. The gardens were the full depth on the northern side of the house and went down to the Drum Stream. It is interesting to note that whilst the north and east elevations of the building are rendered, the south side is built in similar stone to that used in the adjoining building.

It would seem likely that the adjoining building was an integral part of the business and used for storage and the tallow chandlery where candles were manufactured. Tallow is made from rendering beef or mutton fat and this would also have been carried out on the premises. Soap manufacture was often combined with candle making but there is no evidence that soap was made here.

By 1841 the census shows the head of the household as being William Chase, aged 20, with one brother, three sisters, an assistant chandler and three servants. Business must have gone well as by 1861 at the age of 41 he had a wife, Catherine, two daughters, one sister and seven servants living on the premises. They were still grocers and corn merchants, but they were no longer recorded as tallow chandlers.

During the next decade William sold the business to J. P. Cordery, whose family ran it for the next 90 years. John Cordery also prospered during the next decade when he was recorded in 1881 as a grocer and wine merchant with seven children, a governess, a nurse and a servant. The business stayed in the family until early 1950s and was well known as a purveyor of high class groceries and provisions where customers still bought 'over the counter'. The 1881 Census records that J. P. Cordery had also become a wine and spirit merchant and it was to the firm of George Peters, a brewer and wine and spirit merchant from Portsmouth that they sold the business.

One of the first actions that Peters carried out was to sell the adjoining store building, which is now Number 16, to John Gammon. George Peters continued the business as an off-licence until they went into voluntary liquidation in January 1964. The receivers then sold the business and buildings to the London wine merchants, Stowells of Chelsea, who eventually amalgamated with Threshers.

After a hundred years of being an off-licence, by the early 1980s the building had started a new life when it was converted for multi-occupancy. The garden was given over for user car parking with a strip of land alongside the Drum Stream to be used as a public footpath.

Companies known to have occupied the building since 1981 include Seeboard Energy Systems, Computer Scan, Magnet Plumbing and Heating and Heather Grant Studios. The current users are accountants Tarver Deakin and Estate Agents, Homes.

An Eames Clock

This Richard Eames longcase clock was sold at auction by Jacobs and Hunt in Lavant Street and now resides at the home of a local Petersfield farmer.

Richard, living at no. 4 College Street in the 1850s, was the brother of Henry Eames, a renowned clockmaker in the 1860s who was listed in Loomes' book *Watch and Clockmakers of the World*.

20 College Street (White Hart Cottages)

There had been a White Hart Inn at 18/20 High Street since the early 17th century and its grounds extended parallel to College Street (then a turnpike road) as far as the Drum Stream which flows into the Tilmore Brook and beyond into two meadows, known as White Hart Mead and Angel (or Burgess) Mead. Access for horse-drawn vehicles was available from the turnpike road to the outbuildings, by way of what is now Folly Lane. It continued over a bridge and out to College Street.

In 1808, a John Cross of Horndean acquired the leasehold tenure. He built a New White Hart on College Street at the entrance to the private lane and converted no. 18 into a private dwelling, now known as Winton House. The licence was transferred in 1815 to the new White Hart Inn, predecessor to the current premises and many licensees also had other businesses, including two pig dealers, Frances Giles from 1828 to 1839 and John Harding from 1867 to 1878. Mr. Moses recalled that quoits were played by the Petersfield and District Quoits League on the meadow called Moggs Mead in the 1920s, which was accessed by the pathway opposite the White Hart. After play, the participants would retire to the White Hart for refreshments.

To the left of the main building were two detached single storey brick and tiled buildings. Without more detailed investigation it is not possible to ascribe precise dates to them. The first contained stabling and the second had further stabling, subsequently used as a garage, with internal access to a wash-house, with a black kitchen range and a shallow stoneware sink. This latter area may well have been the kitchen to the public house, but became a store room.

When the central car park was developed, all of Burgess Mead and part of what remained of White Hart Mead was acquired by the local authority, together with the strip of land between the then White Hart Inn and no. 22 College Street, which was the top garden of the White Hart. This latter area now forms the exit road from the central car park to College Street.

At the start of the First World War the licensee was Charles Beane but, in 1917, the licence was transferred to his wife, Charlotte, presumably because he had been conscripted. She ran into some difficulties and in May 1919 was fined £1 for selling gin above the maximum price and £1 for not having bottles marked with the maximum price. In 1921 she also received five £5 fines in total for selling intoxicating liquor during prohibited hours and the brewery gave her notice to quit the premises.

No account of the White Hart could be complete without reference to the brewery company responsible for its redevelopment and subsequent liquor supply. It was clearly not accidental that Mr. George Henty, who had once owned several malthouses behind Dragon Street, became interested in the old White Hart. His firm, George Henty & Sons Ltd. at the Westgate Brewery in Chichester, founded in 1893, merged in 1921 with Constable & Son of Arundel, to form Henty & Constable Ltd.

In 1923, Henty & Constable decided to build a 'show-house' and set about demolishing the old White Hart premises and simultaneously building its successor at a cost of £3,000. This involved rebuilding Folly private way to overcome flooding. For its entire 33 year corporate life, from its inception until it ceased brewing in 1954, Henty & Constable owned the White Hart and, during all those years, the Moses family were the licensees.

Albert Moses had been installed as licensee in 1921 after he retired from his First World War service in the Royal Navy. He and his wife Minnie, whom he married in 1898, must have had a tough time keeping the business going whilst the work progressed. At that time, College Street carried all the A3 traffic, north and southbound – and was gravelled! Albert died in 1927 and was succeeded first by his widow, and then by his third son Percival (popularly known as Percy). He and his wife Dorothy, whom he married in 1930, ran the business until 1956, by which time Henty & Constable Ltd. had been succeeded by Friary Holroyd & Healey's Ltd.

In the 1920s and 1930s, farmers' carts and traps were parked along the roadside and the horses stabled for the day in the old buildings to the left of the main building. Later the old stable was opened up as a café and trade was built up for lorry drivers' breakfasts when en route to London from Portsmouth on the A3. The premises were a popular venue for members of the Cyclists' Touring Club as a stop-off point for refreshments. After the Second World War, contracts were negotiated with several coach firms, notably Smith's of Reading, for similar reasons and, regularly, coaches would be parked along the entire frontage as far as Folly Lane.

The Moses partnership pioneered daily bar lunches in the late 1940s, long before food catering in pubs became commonplace and White Hart Catering became a byword for outside catering events such as the Southsea Show, various gymkhanas, agricultural shows, the Leaconfield point-to-point races, farm sales, weddings, various functions at the Town (Festival) Hall and other social gatherings. The café was later named the Bambi Café and was a popular venue for local events.

Although work had been carried out to overcome flooding, the stream still burst its banks from time to time and Mr. Moses put sandbags against the front door, which would hold the water back, but only until a vehicle drove by.

Since that time, over half a century ago, there have been several changes of licensee and a large conservatory was added in later years. Attempts to develop the premises into a motel were frustrated by onerous conditions imposed by the planning authority but permission was granted for the building of eight townhouses, three of which were to incorporate part of the original White Hart building. The development has now been completed and has been named White Hart Cottages.

22 College Street

With its heavily tile-hung elevations, this house now has the appearance of a modern property but was actually built in 1820 and was part of the Jolliffe Estate. The original name of Magdala House has now been restored by the present owner. It stands at an angle to the road as the road curved here when the house was built. A picture taken in 1934 shows Magdala House to the right of the White Hart and the 1911 Census indicates that the property contained six rooms.

In 1891, Frank Waters, aged 28, surveyor to the Urban District Council, was recorded as living here with his wife Agnes, aged 27, and their two sons. However, in 1901, Louis Waters, aged 36 and also a surveyor, was recorded as living here with wife Agnes and two sons. It is possible that Frank had died and Louis and Agnes married for practical reasons, as many people did in this era. Subsequently, Mr. and Mrs. Collis lived here for many years and Jo Collis was particularly well-known in the town as she worked at the Savoy Cinema in Swan Street, while Harold Collis worked for Urquarts motor dealers in Station Road, now White Rose garage.

In the early 1990s, the rear part of the garden was sold for the development of High Willow Flats. In February 2008, permission was granted for a new extension to the north side of the building for a garage and accommodation above and also for a new extension at the rear of the building.

Barham Road

In December 1906, Thomas Wood, a builder whose business was based in Portsmouth, bought a parcel of land stretching from Station Road, behind the properties in College Street and along to where Winton Road is now situated. Included in the strip of land were nos. 24 and 26 College Street, which had been designated to be sold from the Jolliffe estate with the express purpose of opening up a road and building houses along it.

Thomas Wood had been a councillor on the Petersfield Urban District Council from 1901 to 1904 and he was later re-elected in 1907 and served until 1910. He had already built houses in Osborne Road in 1898, and later in Bannerman Road, and the plans for twelve cottages on the south side of Barham Road were submitted in November 1906 and approved.

However, Wood seemed to have been in continuous dispute with the council for his cavalier attitude towards building development. For instance, he put up a building in 1914 on the opposite (north) side of Barham Road which had wooden sides and corrugated iron roofing. This was to be used for storage of materials and for making concrete slabs for houses he intended to erect on adjoining land, but the project was strongly opposed by the council.

In 1915, the council's solicitor had written: 'Although Wood is not an undischarged bankrupt, yet he some time ago executed a Deed of Assignment for the benefit of creditors and he is, I have reason to believe, rather impecunious'. Wood clearly left his mark on Petersfield but it would seem that, in the end, his business venture here ruined him.

24 College Street

These premises are best remembered for Hounsome's Mineral Water Factory. In the 1760s Dr. Joseph Priestly, a scientist and Unitarian Minister, first discovered a method of carbonating water. By the late 18th century carbonated water was being produced commercially.

In 1905, Aubrey Compton started a mineral water business on the premises at 24 College Street, which was shown on maps of the period to have no substantial buildings prior to this, and in 1913 Thomas Hounsome, who was born in 1882, bought the business.

Frank Hounsome, his nephew, lived with his uncle and aunt from 1915 in the then Royal Oak in Sheep Street which had just been rebuilt by Ameys. They used to brew ginger beer, made by adding a halfpennyworth of yeast from Lukers' Brewery to a tub of water containing sugar, acid, cream of tartar and ginger root.

In 1916, he and his uncle went into the army and, as he had to give up the Royal Oak, Thomas Hounsome bought 32 College Street as a home for his wife Ida, who managed the business throughout the war. At the time, she had three small daughters and another was born in August 1916.

After the war, Thomas' sons Edward and Archie joined in the business but Archie later moved to Micheldever and Edward started his own timber business in Holder's Yard at the top of College Street.

At first they had bottles with marbles in that they bought from Redferns of Barnsley. A syrup was made with sugar, water and citric acid, flavoured with essence, then carbonic acid gas was pumped into the bottles under pressure to make the drink fizzy. The bottles were turned upside down and the marble sealed the bottle. They were taken to pubs, off licences and shops, originally on horse drawn drays, but later by van.

At this time they sold only 7- and 10-ounce bottles only at seven pence and nine pence per dozen which retailed at a penny each and there was no deposit charged on the bottle. The business prospered and sidelines were developed. When Mr. Page, the ironmonger at 17 High Street gave up his business before the 1914–1918 war, Thomas Hounsome had taken over his stock-in-trade of marquees and trestle tables. These were stored in Trussler's shed in Dragon Street, at the back of the house next to the Drill Hall. They were used at the Heath Fair where the Hounsomes had a contract for serving lunches and teas.

In the 1920s, Hounsomes took over Fenns of Farnham and so had a wider catchment area, extending from Farnham to Fareham and Odiham to Petworth. They sold Smiths Crisps, which were packed in tins, Bridgewater biscuits and soft drinks made by Schweppes. The firm had two lorries which they used for deliveries. Thomas Hounsome died in November 1926 and the business passed to his widow

Ida who, together with Frank Hounsome, continued to run the business.

There was a circular bottling machine in the area below the syrup room, which was a magnet for wasps in the summer months, and also a belt for labelling the bottles. These were then put into wooden crates for delivery.

Ida Hounsome lived for many years at 2 Barham Road and there was access to the factory via her drive. This was most useful for her as she was confined to a wheelchair in later life.

Ida Hounsome

During the Second World War, many soft drinks businesses closed down. Hounsomes were allowed to continue but had to supply most of their output to the camps and other priority establishments throughout a limited area.

In 1965, the property was sold and Hartridges of Hambledon took over the stock-in-trade. The property was later occupied by an engineering works until Penny Court was built in 2004. This comprises four leasehold flats and a freehold semi-detached house.

The Turnpike

College Street, before the construction of Tor Way and the one-way system in the 1970s, formed part of the A3 London to Portsmouth trunk road. Given the importance of the road, it is therefore strange to find that London-bound travellers from Portsmouth would be met, outside The Old College, with a "T" junction with the Winchester Road, and the need to turn right. Early street plans of this part of Petersfield do not exist. However, John Ogilby's 1675 strip map of the London to Portsmouth highway shows a distinct kink in the road at the northernmost extremity of the built-up area, where a road towards Winchester leads to the west. It may be dangerous to read too much into such a pictorially based small scale map, as some later cartographers show local roads in a bewildering fashion.

However, the first large-scale plan, prepared in 1773 for the Jolliffe properties in Petersfield, clearly shows a configuration instantly recognisable today. The road's current name derives from the original Churcher's College built there in 1729: the earliest relevant deeds held in the Hampshire Record Office dating from 1652 refer to the road as Stoneham Street, but by 1728 it was Stoneham or Cat (sometimes Catt) Street. By 1740, its name had changed to College Street.

With the development of the naval dockyard at Portsmouth, the route from London, through Petersfield, was greatly used. Samuel Pepys, appointed Clerk of the Acts to the Navy Board, a key post in the Royal Dockyard, describes stopping off with his wife, and others, at Petersfield en route to Portsmouth on 1st May 1661, where he was "Up early and baited [i.e. rested] in the room which the King [Charles II] lay in lately at his being there." He described being very merry and playing at bowls. Is it too much to imagine that the King's visits to the town were sufficiently memorable and pleasurable to ennoble one of his mistresses, Louise de Kérouaille, as Baroness Petersfield. Seventeenth and early eighteenth century road travel was perilous: maintenance of roads was a parish responsibility and the burden of the maintenance of the sharp climb over Butser Hill was sorely felt by the local ratepayers. Justices were often called upon to settle disputes over contributions, and petitions to Parliament were raised. In 1710, a petition stated that "...the Highway, leading from Petersfield to the Town of Portsmouth, about Two Miles in Length (by reason of the Multitude of carriages for her Majesty's Service and other Carriages, travelling through that Road) is almost impassable for at least Nine months in every Year." A few months later, on 16th May 1711 Royal Assent was given to an Act of Parliament establishing the Sheet Bridge to Portsmouth Turnpike Trust, the first between London and Portsmouth. (The section north of Sheet was only turnpiked in 1749). The Commissioners appointed by the Act met in Petersfield on 7th June 1711 and by October the turnpikes had been established at both ends. The Act set out the scale of charges: stage coaches drawn by four or more horses were charged a shilling, lighter wagons sixpence each, and every score of hogs five pence. Certain exemptions applied, including soldiers upon their March.

Tollkeepers were unpopular, and, in 1712, one Edward Pratt was prosecuted at the Assizes for breaking the Turnpike and abusing the toll gatherer at Sheet Bridge. The Sheet tollhouse was not immediately erected, and the first toll keeper, Thomas Willard, received an extra weekly wage of three shillings and sixpence for three months pending its construction. But the installation of turnpike gates did not involve immediate road improvements. The cost of road "repairs" from Sheet Bridge to Butser Hill was estimated at £1429.18s.0d, and toll revenues were supplemented by loans to finance this. The section between Petersfield and Sheet, presumably up Ramshill, was in such disrepair that Roger Goldring, the Green Dragon innkeeper and one of two turnpike surveyors, was directed to "forthwith repaire the Road (part of the Highways appointed to be amended by the said Act) between the Black Horse in Petersfield & the Turnpike at Sheetbridge the same being in many places Very Ruinous."

Extract from the London to Portsmouth strip map of John Ogilby, 1675 (north is at the foot of the image)

(Hampshire County Council. Provided by Hampshire Cultural Trust.)

In the early years of the turnpike era, the course of the turnpiked road diverted from its former route from the site of the twentieth century White Hart along what is now Folly Lane to the High Street, at the old White Hart, (now Rowans Hospice Shop and Winton House) to the current straight line past the current Red Lion into Dragon Street. The then landlord of the White Hart, Thomas Swannack, took the opportunity in 1736 to move into premises abutting Dragon Street, diagonally opposite the current Red Lion, calling his establishment "the New White Hart", doubtless with an eye to avoid losing his coaching business in the face of competition from inns directly abutting the new road.

In 1834, the turnpike was generating revenue of over £2600, against its capital indebtedness of nearly £3000, a respectable ratio achieved by few other trusts. The advent of the London to Portsmouth railway line however sounded the death knell for the coaching trade. Whilst the nearest railhead was Alton, and the London to Portsmouth direct lines reached only Godalming, as late as 1857 Robert Crafts at The Red Lion and Dolphin Hotels was advertising regular coach and omnibus services plying to these railheads to meet the trains. In January 1859, the line to Petersfield was opened, giving a direct connexion to London. As with much of the turnpike system nationally, plummeting revenues led to the dismantling of the system. Turnpike gates were pulled down and the maintenance of the highway passed the local highway board in the 1870s with the County Council assuming responsibility in 1888.

26 College Street

This is an interesting property as it was originally two semi-detached houses which belonged to the Jolliffe estate. We cannot be certain when they were built but they both appear on the Petersfield Tithe Map of 1840. On December 31st 1906 these two houses were sold to Thomas Wood, together with land stretching back to what is now Winton Road and behind the properties in College Street up to Station Road, in consideration of a sum of £2000.

Thomas Wood was a town councillor and builder and he built the terraced houses on the south side of Barham Road, and also houses in Osborne Road and North Road, and this parcel of land and the two houses were sold to him from the Jolliffe Estate with the express purpose of building new properties and therefore expanding the town. Old deeds show that "no house fronting proposed road A (Barham Road) on said plan should have a less frontage than 18ft... and of not less value of £200 each exclusive in every case of any stable coachhouse conservatory or other outbuilding."

In the 1901 Census, Richard Macklin lived at no. 26 which had a workshop in the grounds fronting College Street as he had traded as a stonemason. At this time he was listed as being a "mail stable contractor" and no. 24 was occupied by Charles Bulpitt and his wife.

An old postcard (right) shows what was Richard Macklin's house no. 26 on the left, and his workshop next to it. In order to make an entrance from Barham Road onto College Street, the workshop and most of no. 26 were demolished, including the wonderful chimneys. Number 24 became 26 as, by this time, the vacant land to the south of these houses had been occupied by Aubrey Compton's Mineral Water Factory, which became no. 24.

A postcard sent on 1st August 1911 from Clarence Godfrey, a baker in Chapel Street, to his son Roscow Godfrey of no. 26, who was on holiday on the Isle of Wight reads, 'When I sent your postcard last night I forgot to tell you that the men are still in your house and are lightly (sic) to be there for a few days so we are unable to get & do anything', indicating that the alteration work was probably still in progress.

The unusual north elevation was occasioned by the demolition of the major part of the original no. 6. The present owner, who had to make extensive renovations, found that a large beam went right through the north facing wall.

One well known couple, Mr. and Mrs. Fairmaner, lived here for some time. They managed Childs Bookshop in the High Street until it closed in 1965, when they then opened their own bookshop on the corner of Heath Road and Dragon Street. At about this time, no. 26 was named "Homelee" and had a monkey-puzzle tree in the front garden.

Richard Macklin's house with his workshop next door, demolished to make way for Barham Road

28 College Street

Numbers 28, 30 and 32 College Street are slate-roofed double-fronted Victorian villas, each with double-storey bay windows, built in the 1880s.

1882	Thomas Simm
1898	Thomas Clare Jones
1903	Ernest J Thompson
1920	Thomas L Hutson
1923	Charles H Davis
1935	Donald T Chaplin
1940	William A Samuel
1942	Walter Vine
1946	John H Milnes
1954	Edward T C Wheeler

Ministers of the Congregational Church resident at the Manse, 28 College Street

With its façade currently painted pale grey, no. 28 formed the Manse for the then Petersfield Congregational Church (now the United Reformed Church) throughout the first seventy years of its life. The first minister to reside there (1882–1898) was Revd. Thomas Simm, who presided over the opening of the rebuilt chapel building in College Street. In this period the Congregational Church was a thriving religious community.

The Reverend Thomas Clare Jones, author of *Congregationalism in Petersfield – 100th Anniversary. October 26th 1899*, followed him. In the 1901 Census, aged 40, he is listed as resident in the Manse with his wife Annie (31) and their two daughters together with a general servant. His successor, Revd. Ernest James Thompson subsequently went on to accept a call to ministry at the Keswick Ridge Congregational Church, New Brunswick, Canada, and remained in Canada till his death just short of his 99th birthday. Revd. Thomas Lee Hutson, born in 1865, came to the living from the Methodist New Connection, previously living at Watery Lane, Birmingham, with his wife Mary (38) and their son and two daughters. They remained a total of thirteen years in what was described in the 1911 Census as a house with eight principal rooms, before they moved to Emsworth.

On 28th August 1957, the Church resolved to ask the Charity Commissioners for permission to sell the Manse, with a view to purchasing a more modern property. This was granted and the Manse then moved from 28 College Street to a newly-built house in Pulens Crescent, Petersfield.

The new purchaser was Mr. Ron Millar, who initially retained it as a private residence, before forming a dental practice with James Forsyth in the early 1960s. The upstairs of no. 28 was extended to create an office/laboratory and surgery. Messrs. Millar & Forsyth also opened a practice at Waterlooville.

Following their retirement in the early 1970s, the practice was bought by Mike Rapley and Roger Lacey, who continued there under Mr. Rapley (although, unlike Mr. Millar, he resided elsewhere). When Mr. Rapley retired in 2009, the surgery was sold to Mr. A. Khalessi. The building has undergone significant internal updating to offer modern facilities and now trades as the "College Street Dental Centre" offering an extensive range of treatments and dental services.

30 College Street

No. 30 was built circa 1885 and the 1891 Census shows William Wills, a baker born in 1869, living here with his brother George, who was his assistant, and a housekeeper. George Wills was the secretary of Petersfield Football Club and was also a keen Salvationist; by 1907, he was running the business himself and was to be still seen delivering bread around the town in the 1920s.

There was a bakery at the back of the house and this was seemingly in use until the 1950s. Mr. Wills' delivery man, Jimmy Marshall, delivered the bread in a square box on wheels and could often be seen riding on the handles of the cart. At the front of the house there were two rooms upstairs and two rooms downstairs for the family. At the back there was a kitchen and backstairs up to the servant's room. Outside there was a toilet for the servant, a laundry room containing a brick copper and a butler's sink, and a woodshed. Originally there was an entrance to the house from Barham Road as the garden stretched around the back of no. 28. There was also a brick built garage which fronted onto Barham Road which was originally a stable for Mr. Wills' horse and cart.

Later, the property was bought by Mr. and Mrs. Bishop, bakers of Chapel Street, and in 1956 the house was sold to Bill and Millie Pink. They operated a carrier business, Vokes Carrier Service, from the premises and, when they left, this was sold to Door-to-Door Carriers.

The oven in the bakery was the size of a room and a young David Pink, with the help of his grandfather, had to knock out a few bricks every day after school to open up the building. The bakery was used by the Pinks for storage of goods and was converted into an extension of the house – but not attached directly to the main building – at a later date. It is now separately numbered 1B Barham Road, a three-bedroomed property with a vehicular access from Barham Road, and carries the name "The Old Bakehouse".

The Old Bakehouse, Barham Road

College Street a Century Ago

The 1911 Census revealed 40 separate households in College Street, with a total of 149 residents. Whilst purely commercial premises are excluded, three inns appear: The Red Lion, with 26 rooms, The White Hart, with just seven rooms all told, and The Good Intent, at 46a, with six. The largest purely residential properties were Fairley (with 16 rooms), occupied by Dr. Leachman, Churcher's Old College (15 rooms), by Dr. Harry Brownfield, and no. 18 (12 rooms), by grocer John Cordery. The Pines and Cedarcote both had ten rooms. Living-in servants might be expected there, and Cedarcote, Fairley and the Old College housed three, The Pines two, and John Cordery employed one. Two servants lived at Northbrook Cottage, where Charles Money, a retired Naval Officer resided, and one each at nos. 4, 17, and 26.

The oldest householder was 78 year-old farm labourer Robert Cannings, in one of two cottages behind Cedarcote, identified as "Moggs Mead" (a name re-introduced in the 1970s for the Herne Farm spine road). The youngest, both 28 years old, included Charles Flip, innkeeper of The Good Intent. The average age of household heads was 51 years, and 22 were married, six were widows and five widowers. College Street housed a significant number of tradespersons or those in retail trades. Two are directly engaged in food preparation – a cheese manufacturer and a bread baker, as well as a confectioner and a grocer. There were also a watchmaker, a cycle repairer, a boot dealer, and another bootmaker. Shop employees were represented by a grocer's assistant and a florist's manager. More manual trades were reflected by a blacksmith, two bricklayers, and a furniture remover. Domestic servant householders included a charwoman, a laundry ironer, and Dr. Leachman's coachman. Gardeners headed four households, a farm labourer and another skilled labourer one each. Professionals were represented by a practising doctor, two vets, a Congregational Minister and an architect. Retirees comprised a physician, a naval officer, another naval pensioner, and two artisans, a miller and a blacksmith.

The census can reveal when young families moved into the area. Both Dr. Harry Brownfield, at the Old College, and his wife, were Londoners, but all their children (the eldest born in 1891) were native to Petersfield. Although thirteen householders were born within a five-mile radius of Petersfield, Charles Money was born aboard ship, and Louise Bowden Smith in Calcutta. Of 22 householders' wives, eight were born within five miles of Petersfield, and one each from as far afield as Yorkshire and Ireland. The most substantial accommodation occupied by a locally-born man was that of the watchmaker William Bradley. The larger, solely residential properties were occupied without exception by incomers to the Petersfield area.

CENSUS OF ENGLAND AND WALES, 1911.

Name and Surname	Relationship to Head of Family	Age (Males)	Age (Females)	Condition as to Marriage	Completed years present Marriage	Children born alive	Children still living	Children who have died	Personal Occupation	Birthplace
Albert Leachman	Head	72		Married					Retired Physician	London Islington
Louisa Leachman	Wife		67	Married	45	6	4	2		Wilts. Westbury
Mildred Leachman	Daughter		42	Single						Hants. Petersfield
Janet Leachman	Daughter		39	Single						Hants. Petersfield
Minnie Stanton	Servant		24	Single					Cook Servant (Domestic)	Wilts East Knoyle
Mabel Rope	Servant		22	Single					Servant (Domestic)	Norfolk Norwich
[illegible] Gregory	Servant		17	Single					Servant (Domestic)	Hants. East Meon

16

Signature A.W. Leachman

Postal Address Fairley, Petersfield

The 1911 Census entry for Fairley

The Petersfield Tithe Map and Award

Although prior maps exist, such as that prepared in 1773 for John Jolliffe (right) to identify his properties, the earliest and most comprehensive survey of the town took place in 1840 in connection with the Tithe Award.

The purpose of the 1836 Tithe Act was to substitute money payments for payments in kind, and detailed parish plans were required to identify land areas and uses. That for Petersfield covered the entire 234 acres and 23 perches, and resulted in a total town annual monetary tithe of £50. Tithes were by then no longer payable for some properties, so the award for the town does not provide a full schedule of owners and occupiers, and large numbers of individual buildings, particularly in the centre of the town, are therefore grouped together in one parcel number.

The combination of the map and the award, which legally comprised one document, however, provides valuable information about the nature of College Street at the beginning of the Victorian era.

College Street Properties Subject to Tithe

Parcel Number	Size	Landowner	Occupier	Description and State of Cultivation
15	1 acre 0 rods 24 perches	Sir William Jolliffe	Richard Brewer and others	House and Nursery
16	1 acre 0 rods 32 perches	Sir William Jolliffe	Anthony Aldridge	Arable
17	1 acre 0 rods 32 perches	Sir William Jolliffe	Richard Brewer and others	House, Malthouse etc.
19	1 rod 20 perches	Churcher's College	George Dusautoy	House, School etc.
21	20 perches	Charles Greetham	Alfred Dusautoy and others	Cottages and Gardens
22	8 perches	Robert Parsons	John Lambert and others	House and Garden
23	23 perches	Mary Greenwood	Mary Greenwood	House and Garden
52	2 acres 2 rods 18 perches	Samuel Andrews	John Chase	Moggs Meadow Pasture
53	1 rod 4 perches	Samuel Andrews	John Chase	House and Garden
54	3 rods 8 perches	Sir William Jolliffe	Richard Brewer and others	House and Nursery
55	2 acres	Sir William Jolliffe	John Lipscombe	Pasture

Houses etc.

Parcel Number	Size	Description in Award
14	7 acres 3 rods	Houses north of High Street
18	1 acre 2 rods 14 perches	Houses College Street
20	1 rod 8 perches	Meeting House and Yard
24	1 acre 1 rod 2 perches	College Street
25	1 acre 2 rods 27 perches	East side of College Street including Red Lion

Tithe Map of Petersfield 1841

32 College Street

This is the third of three examples of late Victorian domestic architecture, built at the same time as numbers 28 and 30, circa 1885. The 1901 and 1891 Census records show that George Pond, a black-smith, and his wife Elizabeth were living here but in 1911 the occupant was George Pond, a widower. Ida Hounsome lived here with her family from 1916 while her husband, Thomas Hounsome, was serving during the First World War. During this time she was managing the family business, the Hounsome Mineral Water factory, at 24 College Street.

The will of Frederick Ward, a retired pianoforte dealer, shows that he was living here in 1940 and probate was obtained in August 1941.

During the 1950s, Miss Bell and Miss Blake, proprietors of Madame Lynne dress shop in the High Street, were the occupants and their shop occupied the building which is now the Cancer Research shop.

In 2007, planning permission was granted to demolish a single-storey flat-roofed extension at the rear and replace it with a two-storey pitched roof extension.

34 College Street

Old maps indicate that this property, set back from the road in contrast with the later Victorian villas nearby, was built between 1840 and 1870. Census records indicate that Helen Blackmore, a dressmaker, was living there in 1891 with two lodgers. In 1901, the occupants were Alfred Waller, a road foreman, and his wife Ruth, and they had one boarder.

The 1911 Census shows that the house now comprised two households: the larger original portion was numbered 34a and was occupied by William Denyer, a domestic gardener, his wife Mary, and their two sons.

A smaller, single-storey, two-roomed building at the back, numbered 34b, was occupied by Alfred Waller, a widower who, at the age of 74, was a jobbing gardener. The present owner found brickwork from this small building when excavating for his extension in 2011. There had also been a water supply to the modest additional building, thus suggesting that working people of that era with few financial resources were grateful for any accommodation rather than go to the workhouse and that they were also prepared to work into old age.

The most recent extension to the property was made in 2011, when a two-storey extension was added at the rear of the house.

36a, 36, and 38a College Street

No. 36a

No. 36

No. 38a

This building, in common ownership until the latter part of the 20th century, now forms three individual private properties, the core of which represents one of the oldest surviving structures in College Street. The precise division into three residences, and particularly between numbers 36 and 38a appears somewhat artificial as the central cottage, No. 36, includes some of the flint and brick faced structure immediately abutting the pavement shared with No. 38a. Viewing the properties from the road, left to right (south to north), nos. 36a and 36 are Grade II listed.

The 17th century frontage of 36 and 36a College Street, dating from about 1640 and set back from the current pavement, comprises a wide but shallow three-bay timber-framed construction typical of the homes of Wealden rural yeomen. Original exposed beams exist in all the rooms. The structure is half-timbered with thin bricks (1.5ins thick); some of the lower walls are constructed of three thicknesses of brick and two tiles on edge resulting in a solid wall of 18ins thickness. The oak timbers are still in good condition. Number 36 exhibits a bewildering variation in floor levels, perhaps unsurprising as the recollection of Peter Hann from over 50 years ago is that much of a narrow section of the rear elevation at ground floor level, only a few feet deep, then comprised separate rooms: an apple store, a larder and a kitchen.

The hipped roof is of clay tiles and the first floor is fish-scale tile-hung, with a central brick chimney. The rear of the property has three gabled dormer windows in a long pent roof.

Little is known of the early history of the building, but, by the 1840s, it was part of the Jolliffe estate, and was occupied by Richard Brewer and others, and its use at the time of the Tithe Award was that of a "House, Malthouse, etc." This is perhaps unsurprising, as within what is now no. 36 are the remains of a funnel-like structure, once about ten feet square, a former drying kiln for barley stored in the loft above. The whole property was contained within a plot of just over an acre, which, behind the bustle of College Street, remained into the 20th century a peaceful orchard garden and croquet lawn.

By 1891 the property was owned by South Eastern Farmers Limited and it is reasonable to suggest that a census entry of 1881 for a corn dealer, John Hunt, relates to the building. Ten years later it was occupied by James Marshall, a baker, his wife and five children under the age of nine. The Marshall family continued in residence until after the end of the First World War. The three properties had been purchased

The Hann family

by Harry Hann, a tinsmith and ironmonger for his business and domestic use for himself, his wife and five children. There was a bakehouse in the garden of what is now no. 38a, and also a well 40 feet in depth. In later years, the bakehouse was demolished and the well was filled in. A second well, the top of which can be seen in the centre of the front garden of no. 36, was filled in during the 1970s.

The two-storey brick and flint hipped roof building, directly abutting the pavement, became a shop and workshop for the business, with a tinsmith's store at first floor level in the northernmost section, whilst the first floor of the southern section contained a bedroom and bathroom accessed from what is now no. 36. Attached to the side of this building was a (now demolished) single-storey extension which Harry Hann's wife and daughter ran as a general store, a use that continued for over 30 years. The tinsmith trade involved what might today be regarded as heavy industrial activity, chiefly concerned with the re-tinning of milk churns. A steel flue pipe was constructed from the furnace on the ground floor, through the store and the roof above. From 1923, half the shop area was dedicated to the trade of a tinsmith and, on market days, local farmers would buy their milking pails and chicken troughs there. In the meantime, Harry Hann was also trading as a plumber and heating engineer.

The rest of the property had been divided in 1936 when the layout was altered at the southern end to provide separate accommodation for Harry Hann's married daughter. This became 36a College Street, also known as Cat Cottage at this time, a reference to the former name for College Street.

During the late 1960s, the local demand for repairing metalwork had diminished and the Hann family decided to sell the whole property and the Wadham Stringer Garage Group acquired it. Amongst their interests in Petersfield was a car showroom on the adjacent land that now forms Cremorne Place. In 1976, they applied for planning permission to use the building in College Street for light industry. The application was refused because 'it would be visually detrimental to the street scene and adversely affect the setting of nearby listed buildings.' Three years later, the Wadham Stringer Group sought permission to demolish the building to erect a car showroom and offices for the company. Planning permission was again refused on the grounds that the building was of particular historical interest and would damage the character of this part of College Street, and in 1979 most of the building was given the protection of listed building status.

It was considered that the building should be made fit for re-occupation and B & P Estate Management were granted planning permission in 1983 to convert the whole building into three individual dwellings, two with much truncated rear gardens, and in 1985 this conversion was completed to create the three properties as they are today.

29–30 Cremorne Place

This space was formerly the entrance to the Wadham Stringer Garage, but, in 1995 when Cremorne Place, a complex of apartments for retired people in neighbouring King George Avenue, was built on the site of the garage, two maisonettes were built facing onto College Street. These are numbered as part of Cremorne Place with a private access path between them and The Good Intent.

There is an old wall attached to the end of no. 38a, which is the remains of a three storey brick and flint building, originally Henry Houghton-Brown's walking stick factory.

Subsequently, it became a cheese factory and, in the 1950s, it was a wholesale grocery store, the proprietors being W. L. Palmer Ltd.

The old wall adjacent to 38a College Street seen from the south.

House numbering

Any attempt to make complete sense of historical records before the late 19th century, and College Street is no exception, is met with the absence of street numbering. Indeed, the first census showing house numbers for College Street was that of 1901. The earliest known system for identifying individual houses in Petersfield had emerged with postal services stimulated by the 17th century coaching trade.

A piecemeal house-numbering system in Petersfield was developed, doubtless for ease of rent collection, by the Lords of the Manor, the Jolliffes, in the early 19th century. Their properties in Sheep Street, totalling about 40 houses, were each identified by numbers attached to the underside of doorway hoods and some can still be seen today. With the departure of the Jolliffes in 1911, these numbers ceased to have any significance.

In the late 18th century, a central distribution point for letters had first been set up in the High Street at the (old) White Hart (now number 20, Rowans' Hospice). Before moving to its current location in the Square in 1922, the "Post Office" had for 30 years been located in a substantial building in the High Street, at what is now the site of Michael Miller and Partners' Funeral Services. Prior to this, relocation of the town's postal service had been a constant feature. Certainly from the early 1840's, a Post Office existed at 4 College Street, and the 1851 Census shows Richard Eames as a sub-distributor of stamps. There is an 1855 directory entry in similar terms, but by the 1861 Census, Richard is employed in Henry Eames clockmaker's business.

Doorway hood in Sheep Street

40–46 College Street (The Good Intent)

The Good Intent and its adjacent cottages originally comprised a classic 17th century house of 3½ bays with a lobby entry. It was typical of many rural houses once referred to as "yeoman's farmhouses", which had small-panel framing, lobby entry and a back-to–back chimney stack, with one room on either side of the chimney. The joists, spine beams and down braces suggest a date of c.1650–1675.

A further two timber-framed bays were added to the north and the south of the main building at a later date, but the partition walls of these additions were destroyed in the 18th century, when the whole structure became a row of small one-up and one-down cottages.

There are no very early records of The Good Intent as an alehouse, but the cottages were probably occupied by beer retailers. The premises once also housed a malthouse. In The Inns of Petersfield published by The Petersfield Area Historical Society in 1977, the authors write: "In old Petersfield, there were houses which seem to have switched from private dwelling to alehouse and back again, and it is difficult to be sure what their status was at any given date. Indeed, there is reason to think that, especially in the period 1660–1760, a number of substantial citizens from time to time set aside a part of the dwelling house for public drinking without formally entering the trade."

The information provided by the censuses of 1841 to 1911 reveal that The Good Intent had at least eight changes of ownership in the seventy year period: only Thomas Bone, listed as Maltster and Brewer, and his wife held the tenancy for longer than ten years, and the rest were generally labelled as innkeepers. In all cases, their families lived with them and, in the instance of Charles Matchem, in 1871, this included three sons and four daughters. It is clear, therefore, that the whole property was considered as a family house and concern.

The northern addition (now constituting the main College Street entrance to the pub) had a cross-bay added in the 20th century and the pub has gradually absorbed all the cottages as they have become vacant.

In 1916, when The Good Intent was owned by the local family of Lukers, an objection was raised to the licence held by Mrs. Fripp, a widow with five

children. In fact, at the time, Petersfield could boast of thirteen licensed houses and three beerhouses, an average of one such establishment to every 247 inhabitants! During the First World War, an upstairs room was known as "the soldiers' room" as it housed half a dozen Seaforth Highlanders who were in transit to the fighting in France.

Until the late 19th century, Petersfield had had four local breweries and a strong supporting industry of hop growers in the vicinity. The Good Intent was a Luker house, owned by the brewing family whose brewery stood at the other end of College Street. The Good Intent was taken over by Strong & Co., brewers of Romsey in 1934, when it took over the Red Lion after Lukers' Brewery fire.

After the sale of The Good Intent by the Strongs chain to Whitbreads, it became a free house. Although one tenant held the licence there for 40 years, the post Second World War period saw a shift in the pattern of ownership, with several families taking charge of the inn for only short periods of time, one couple being the landlords for a mere 16 months.

Whitbreads even once threatened that if they could not find a licensee for the premises, they would sell it as a private house.

In the 1960s, a small space was discovered within a chimney stack between the pub and the neighbouring cottage. As has often been the case with this property, the discovery fuelled speculation about the tiny room's possible used as a smugglers' den or illicit store for highwaymen's contraband – or even a priest's hole, but, sadly, there were no clues as to its real origins.

Another colourful (literally) episode occurred in the 1970s, when the then licensees, John and Judy Sparrow, decided to paint the outside of the building pink (strictly "rose madder"). Despite protests from many quarters, the colour was justified by reference to a book by the Duke of Gloucester on the revival of historic house colours by the Sandtex firm of paint manufacturers, and the colour remained until the 1980s.

Keith Gibson, the previous licensee (who had run the pub as a bistro named "Fatties"), had installed bathrooms in the nos. 40-46 College Street properties and a kitchen for the pub. The new licensees, the Sparrows, started cream teas as well as offering a fine selection of real ales and the first bed and breakfast accommodation at the pub.

As extra space from the incorporation of the adjacent cottages became available, a restaurant was added and the building became the premises we still know today, with its outside eating area as well as seating for around fifty diners inside the restaurant. It continues to offer bed and breakfast facilities and holds music events several times a week.

This is why the planners saw red

East Hampshire District Planners saw red, or rather a shade of raspberry pink when the new owner of the Good Intent public house at Petersfield decided to repaint the exterior of the beamed building.

Months later the Council's Planning Committee decided repainting an architecturally listed building needed special consent and by six votes to five gave authority for legal proceedings to be taken against John and Judy Sparrow, owners of the 16th Century coaching inn on the A3 Portsmouth to London road.

Planning Officer Mr. A. R. Billeness, at Alton, said: "Before we do that we are requesting the owner to make a belated application for listed building consent. Then the matter can be considered further."

The owner, Mr. John Sparrow, said he had been approached to make an application but wondered if by doing this he would be admitting legally that he was guilty of an offence.

"It is all so petty and the Council has gone completely the wrong way about it," he told a reporter. "When we started the painting, if someone had come across and told me I was making a big mistake with the colour, I would have listened.

"It is now six months later and the first I hear about the business is when a reporter phones me after a planning committee meeting.

"Quite honestly, we don't like the Council's attitude. They seem to think we have deliberately slapped on some terrible flashy colour to attract business.

The colour, called Rose Madder, was one of a set of old British pigments in use before the Norman Conquest, now being marketed by a paint company especially for old buildings, he said.

The Council h referred to the colour "deep mulberry" one member Mr. L. Sandford (Clanfield Buriton) called "psychedelic and qu dreadful."

The last word ca from Mrs. Judy Sparr who admitted the co was "a bit brighter" they anticipated.

A Rose Madder by other name . . . and Hampshire Telegraph colour, allows you to for yourself.

HT 2

46a College Street

This property consists of a residence and an adjacent workshop, both fitting architecturally and sympathetically with their surroundings. They are, however, not contemporaneous with the properties on either side, but have been so designed to suit the immediate neighbours.

The authors are grateful to Edward Roberts for his architectural assessment of the building which follows:

"The main (residential) property is now a two-storey house which clearly did not start life as a domestic building; it has no original chimney and there are too few original windows for a house of this size. The interior timbers do not indicate original partitions and the whole was probably built as a store or workshop – perhaps with no upper floor. There is a break in a side wall (now blocked) that may represent a very narrow door, but it is probable that originally there was a wide entrance facing the road. The brick walls, which are of good quality and laid in Flemish bond, are consistent with a 19th century date.

The adjacent workshop (fronting directly onto the pavement) also probably dates back to the 19th century. Its flint walls, where they survive, imply a lower status than the brick building. It seems always to have had an upper floor and was probably a store with both floors originally open to the courtyard. It is a workaday structure that has been patched over the years and has been given a new roof at some stage in its life."

Research in the census records shows that a Thomas Summers had lived here with his wife Emma from about 1871 until 1901. His occupation was that of a "ropemaker" and this coincides with the local belief that the house was once called "The Rope Walk". It is entirely feasible that the workshop building was given over to ropemaking during this period and that Thomas Summers was the owner both during his working lifetime and later during his retirement.

By the 1911 Census, however, the premises had become the home of Harry Morris, who was a skilled labourer with the G.P.O. (General Post Office). He also had a lodger at the time.

Queen Elizabeth in College Street Traffic Jam

This is the only known photograph of Queen Elizabeth II in Petersfield. It was taken in August 1953, her coronation year, when the Queen passed through the town on her way to Spithead for the Review of the Fleet ceremony, just as many previous monarchs had done in centuries past. The royal entourage passed a smartly executed "present arms" by the Churcher's College CCF who were lining Ramshill.

Unfortunately, the royal Rolls Royce came to a momentary, unofficial halt in College Street (then two-way) when its passage was blocked by a coach driving in the opposite direction. Hence this photo-opportunity.

48 College Street

Although undoubtedly the oldest extant house in Petersfield, its true antiquity is hidden from view in its internal roof timbering and a wattle-and-daub partition in the attic. However, its age is revealed by its 14th century crown post roof parallel to the street. Multiple re-designing over the centuries has thus concealed its origins, and Georgian brickwork completes the encasement of the whole, lending it an 18th century "feel", with its projecting centre and flat parapet probably inspired by, and matching that of, Churcher's Old College opposite.

Edward Roberts' own, more detailed, description, refers to the two visible bays being probably two thirds of an original three-bay house, with a third bay or cross-wing now missing. The rather inelegant crown-post roof is similar to others in central Hampshire that date to the late 14th century. The southern bay of the house was originally an open hall in which smoke from an open hearth rose to deposit soot on the rafters above. The projecting brick stack of 1660 is evidence that, by that date, the open hall had been sealed over so that the hall needed to be heated by a brick chimney. The roof over the "hall" (to the left of the front door) is still sooted. In the rear wing of the house behind the "parlour" (to the right of the front door) there is a queen-strut roof of the late 15th century.

Sadly, little is known of the building's owners over the centuries. Its position on the edge of the old hamlet of Stoneham suggests that a prosperous tenant farmer occupied it with his family. Their farm would have surrounded the property, stretching from the boundary with Petersfield to a point located in the neighbouring village of Sheet. Subsequently, the building was occupied by tradespeople such as Thomas Summers, the ropemaker, whose large family lived here in the latter half of the nineteenth century.

Several alterations took place in Victorian times, but also later in 1904 and 2006, when it was owned respectively by two local building firms: the Gammons (late 19th century) and the Holders (20th). Shortly before the First World War, no. 48 became the home of the veterinary surgeon, John Boxall and his family, when it contained eight rooms, including Mr. Boxall's surgery.

More recently, it was owned and inhabited by Richard Holder, one of the many members of the Holder family to live in this part of College Street, who wrote his own *Theoretical History of 48 College Street* in 2005. As an active member of the Victorian Society, he ensured the sympathetic conservation and repair to the property. His contribution towards retaining the original historic fabric of the house was exemplary and some of the poor brickwork on the southern and western sides of the building was replaced by the Society, as were some internal floors and ceilings.

50 and 52 College Street (formerly "The Black Horse")

The first record of the Blackhorse, previously the Shoulder of Mutton, is in 1709 when John Jinman, who had inherited the property from his father, leased a fourth to Allwyn Palmer. John Jinman was described as a victualler and the property was divided into four and each part leased separately. His will, dated 8th November 1740, also described him as a victualler and he left the property to his wife Katharine for her lifetime and, on her death, a fourth of the property to his brother Nicholas and a fourth each to his three nieces, Anne March, Jane March and Mary Tozy.

After his death John Jinman's widow Katharine married Joseph Grant who took over as victualler. Each fourth of the house was leased, usually for one year at a time, the rent in 1742 being £20 to £30. In 1741 Elizabeth Barnard, a widow, sublet the back kitchen and the drink house, or little cellar, for five shillings and one peppercorn on the Day of St. Thomas. The property must have been a hive of activity with various tenants and ale house customers coming and going.

The Jolliffe family had already established a foothold in the town and Sir William Jolliffe stood down as member of Parliament in favour of his nephew John Jolliffe in 1741. By this time Katharine must have died as Joseph Grant purchased three fourths of the property from the nieces of John Jinman and sold them to John Jolliffe on 26th December 1743 for £30 and a lease back to him for one thousand years at a rent of one shilling per year. This was important for Jolliffe as the mayor persisted in his refusal to disallow votes for split tenements.

The next record that we find, the census of 1841, shows that the property is now two dwellings and is no longer an alehouse. Number 50 was occupied by Robert Wetherspoon, a bricklayer, and number 52 by John Spencer, a carter. The census of 1911 shows that number 50a, four rooms, was occupied by Elizabeth Marshall, a widow and that 50b, one room, was occupied by Harry Weston. Number 52, four rooms, was occupied by Luke Loader. Therefore the Blackhorse had nine rooms divided into four dwellings.

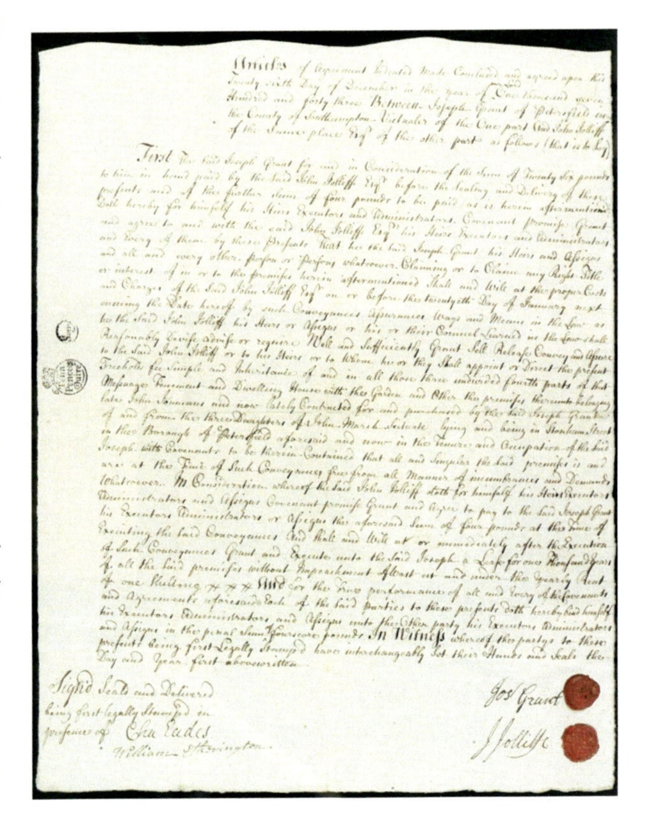

Articles of Agreement Indented Made Concluded and agreed upon the twenty sixth Day of December in the year of [our Lord] One thousand seven Hundred and forty three Between Joseph Grant of Petersfield in the County of Southampton Victualer of the One part And John Jolliff of the same place Esq of the other part as follows (that is to say)

First The said Joseph Grant for and in Consideration of the Sum of Twenty six pounds to him in hand paid by the said John Jolliff Esq before the Sealing and Delivery of these presents and of the further sum of four pounds to be paid as is herein aftermentioned Doth hereby for himself his Heirs Executors and Administrators Covenant promise Grant and agree to and with the said John Jolliff Esq his Heirs Executors and Administrators and Every of them by these Presents That he the said Joseph Grant his Heirs and Assigns and all and every other person or persons whatsoever Claiming or to Claim any Right Title or interest of in or to the premises herein aftermentioned Shall and Will at the proper Costs and Charges of the said John Jolliff Esq on or before the twentyeth Day of January next ensuing the Date hereof by such Conveyances Assurances Ways and Means in the Law as he the said John Jolliff his Heirs or Assigns or his or their Counsel Learned in the Law shall Reasonably Devise advise or require Well and Sufficiently Grant Sell Release Convey and Assure to the said John Jolliff or to his Heirs or to Whome he or they Shall appoint or Direct the present Freehold fee Simple and Inheritance of and in all those three undivided fourth parts of that Messuage Tenement and Dwelling House with the Garden and Other the premises thereunto belonging late John Jinmans and now lately Contracted for and purchased by the said Joseph Grant of and from the three Daughters of John March Situate lying and being in [illegible] Street in the Borough of Petersfield aforesaid and now in the Tenure and Occupation of the said Joseph with Covenants to be therein Contained that all and Singular the said premises is and are at the Time of Such Conveyances free from all Manner of incumbrances and Demands Whatsoever. In Consideration whereof the said John Jolliff doth for himself his Heirs Executors Administrators and Assigns Covenant promise Grant and Agree to pay to the said Joseph Grant his Executors Administrators or Assigns the aforesaid Sum of four pounds at the time of Executing the said Conveyances And Shall and Will at or immediately after the Execution of such Conveyances Grant and Execute unto the said Joseph a Lease for one thousand years of all the said premises without Impeachment of Wast at and under the yearly Rent of one Shilling x x x And for the true performance of all and Every of the Covenants and Agreements aforesaid Each of the said parties to these presents doth hereby bind himself his Executors Administrators and Assigns unto the Other party his Executors Administrators and Assigns in the penal Sum of fourscore pounds In Witness whereof the partys to these presents being first Legally Stamped have interchangeably Set their Hands and Seals the Day and Year first abovewritten

Signed Sealed and Delivered being first legally Stamped in presence of Chr [illegible]
William Etherington

Jos Grant
J Jolliffe

The indenture of sale of the property to John Jolliffe, 1743

The Commutation of Tithes Act led to the Petersfield Tithe Awards of 31st August, 1841 which apportioned rent in lieu of tithes to the Reverend Charles Gower Boyles, incumbent of the chapelry , and owner of all the tithes in Petersfield. The total rent was set at £50, divided between owners of arable land, meadow or pasture, common land and buildings and gardens. The discharge from tithes took place on 1st October 1841 and the first rent payment was due within 6 months.

Property no. 18, as shown on the Tithe Map of 1840, encompasses all the properties from Station Road to the Good Intent and in the Tithe Awards this is shown as being owned by Jolliffe Sir William George Hylton Bart. When the Jolliffe estate sold the property the first purchaser was a member of the Gammon family and was later sold to a member of the Holder family. Andrew Gammon (1833–1916), son of Thomas Gammon (1801–1866), was a builder and decorator and he married three times, the third wife being Alice Holder.

Although the property has been let to tenants for several years, it is now back in the occupancy of a member of the Holder family.

The original inn sign painted onto the wall is still visible but barely legible today. It reads:
THE BLACK HORSE
LICENSED TO SELL BEERS AND SPIRITS

The Drum Stream

As you drive along College Street, it is not obvious that you pass over a culvert through which flows the Drum Stream, one of the three streams of Petersfield. The stream rises in fields to the north of the Winchester Road near Stroud and then flows east through ditches and culverts and is fully visible along the length of the central car park before passing through a 35-metre-long culvert under College Street between White Hart Cottages and the boundary wall of Cedar Court. It then flows on for a short distance before joining Tilmore Brook, flowing eastwards through Herne Farm, before reaching the River Rother near Penns place.

A map from 1773 shows no indication of a bridge over the stream at College Street, neither is there any written mention of it, so it reasonable to assume that a culvert was in place and had been since the road was reconstructed when the turnpike road was built in 1711.

During the first half of the 20th century, the stream caused severe flooding on several occasions, notably in January 1928 when melting snow and torrential rain brought the worst flooding in the town for nearly half a century. College Street was flooded from the entrance to Barham Road down to The Red Lion. In the vicinity of The White Hart and Lukers Brewery, it was reported as three to four feet deep. In 1953, heavy flooding was again recorded in College Street, with water entering The White Hart.

The problems and damage caused by flooding had been of great concern to the authorities for many years and archives indicate that the Town and Highways surveyor was actively involved in seeking a solution over a long period. Following the floods of 1953, reports were commissioned from various agencies including the West Sussex River Board. It appears that, thankfully, a solution was eventually found by various improvements being made at different places along the stream.

52a College Street (Holders' Yard)

This corner site, where the north-west end of College Street meets Station Road (formerly Cow Legs Lane), was once occupied by a building which must have been constructed between 1793 (as shown by the map of Lord Stawell's properties) and 1840 (indicated on the Tithe Map). By this time, the site had become the property of the Gammons, the chief Petersfield building firm during the Victorian period. Several members of the Gammon family, listed in the censuses as carpenters or builders, also lived in College Street for a large part of the 19th century.

The Holder family

The whole of this corner yard site, including the late 18th century barn standing further back from Station Road and the nearby Edwardian brick-built engine house (with chimney), stands as a symbol of the unbroken commercial connection with two major Petersfield building firms – first, the Gammons and later, the Holders – over nearly two hundred years. The monogram (containing the initials J, G & S – John Gammon and Son) on the front facade of no. 52a College Street attests to this ownership.

Both the building firms of Gammons and Holders needed large premises within the town for such associated trades as timber sawing, cart mending, scaffolding and wheel and shaft building and repairs, for which a large work and storage space was essential. The barn is the oldest and only remaining such premises still in existence in Petersfield. The engine house is a historic relic of the later stage of development in these trades – and their use of engines to drive the machinery required by their work practices.

Sadly, in 1904, there was a fire at the Gammons' workshops in the yard which destroyed one portion of the ancient barn. Three years later, John Gammon died and the property was bought by the Holder family, in whose ownership the yard and adjacent houses (nos. 50 and 52) have remained for over a century.

In recent years, the barn has been used by various businesses as a workshop and storage area, thereby retaining the traditional uses of the buildings. When Gwen Holder recently died, the property was handed down to her daughter who is seeking permission to develop the whole site. The end property, no. 52a, is currently called The Wishing Well, an osteopathic practice with its associated offices.

Resources & Acknowledgements

Sources, references and acknowledgments

PROPERTIES (EAST)
The Red Lion and the Old Masonic Hall: www.britishlistedbuildings.co.uk; HRO Finding 21M64; Report of the Case of the Borough of Petersfield, R. S. Atcheson, (ed.), 1831; www.historyofparliamentonline.org/volume/1820-1832/constituencies/petersfield
No. 15: (Northbrook): Taylor Collection (LSE); Greenwich Maritime Museum; Jess Jenkins
No. 17: Edward Roberts
United Reformed Church: Petersfield URC Minute books and archive; The United Reformed Church (Wessex) Trust Ltd.; Jean Hounsome; Peter Jolly; HRO Finding 91A02
Churcher's Old College: Nathaniel Atcheson (1823); J. H. Smith (1936); Brooks and Clarke (2007); Jill Walker; Richard Brownfield; Paul Fisher

PROPERTIES (WEST)
Nos. 10-12: Jerry Hicks; David Jeffery
Nos. 16-18: John Gammon; David Jenvey; Chris Jacobs
No. 20: (White Hart Cottages): Moses family archive
No. 24: Jean Hounsome; Roger Lacey; Colin Emmins; Photographs by: Robert Smallbone, Frederick Smallbone
No. 26: Tom Norgate; Teresa Murley; Diana Syms
No. 30: David Pink
No. 32: Jean Hounsome; David Pink
Nos. 36a, 36, 38a: Peter Hann; Margaret Hawkes
No. 48: Richard Holder; Edward Roberts; Michael Bullen
No. 52a: Jean Hounsome; Sheila Bowler

Other general sources consulted

Tithe Map: HRO Finding 21M65/F7/187/2
Censuses: www.nationalarchives.gov.uk; www.ancestry.co.uk; www.findmypast.co.uk
Newspapers: *Petersfield Post*; *Petersfield Herald*; *Hampshire Chronicle*
Hampshire Treasures: Hampshire County Council: Hampshire Treasures Online, Vol. 6
Trade and historical directories: Pigot's; Kelly's; White's; Post Office
Victoria County History: British History Online, Vol. 3: Petersfield Parish, 1908
History, Gazetteer and Directory of Hampshire and the Isle of Wight (1859)
(specialcollections.le.ac.uk/cdm/)
The Petersfield Index: Petersfield Library (Local History Section), publ.: PAHS, Vol I (1997); Vol 2 (2004)
Parish registers (online resource) and Hampshire Record Office
Petersfield Area Historical Society (PAHS): *Bulletins*; *Monographs*; *Petersfield Papers*